PUBLISHED IN THE STREETS OF DHAKA:
COLLECTED POEMS

By The Same Author
Poetry:

Starting Lines: Poems 1968-75 (Dhaka: Liberty 1978)

A Little Ado: Poems 1976-77 (Dhaka: Granthabithi 1978)

A Happy Farewell (Dhaka: University Press Limited 1994)

Black Orchid (London: Aark Arts 1996)

The Logopathic Reviewer's Song (Dhaka: University Press Limited and London: Aark Arts 2002)

Published in the Streets of Dhaka: Collected Poems 1966-2006 (Dhaka: writers.ink, 2007)

Selected Poems of Shamsur Rahman (translation) (Dhaka: BRAC 1985, enlarged edition, Pathak Samabesh 2007)

Contemporary Indian Poetry (editor) (Columbus: Ohio State University Press 1990)

Padma Meghna Jamuna: Modern Poetry from Bangladesh (editor) (Delhi: Foundation of South Asian Writers and Literature, 2009)

Calcutta 1971 and Other Poems, translated into Oriya from Kaiser Haq's original English by Dr. Sangram Jena (Bhubaneswar: Arya Vedanta Publications, 2010)

Prose Translations:

Quartet (Rabindranath Tagore's Chaturanga) (Oxford: Heinemann 1993, also in Tagore Omnibus Vol. I, Penguin India 2006, and Classic Rabindranath, Penguin India, 2011)

The Wonders of Vilayet (an 18th century Indian's travel memoir) (Leeds: Peepal Tree Press 2002; Delhi: Chroniclebooks, 2008; Dhaka: Writers.Ink, 2012)

The Perfect Model and Other Stories by Anis Choudhury (Dhaka: writers.ink, 2010)

The Woman Who Flew (Nasreen Jahan's Urukku) (Delhi: Penguin India, 2012)

PUBLISHED IN THE STREETS OF DHAKA

Collected Poems

WITH NEW POEMS INCLUDING " ODE ON THE LUNGI"

For Norman & Susie
with love
Kaiser Haq

Kaiser

Ⓤⓟ The University Press Limited

The University Press Limited
Red Crescent House
61 Motijheel C/A, G. P. O. Box 2611
Dhaka 1000, Bangladesh
Phone: 9565441, 9565444
Fax: 8802 956 5443
E-mail: upl@bangla.net, upl@btcl.net.bd
Website: www.uplbooks.com

First Published 2012

Cover design by Amal Das
Cover photograph by Zubair Khan Copper

ISBN 978 984 506 113 1

Published by Mohiuddin Ahmed, The University Press Limited, Dhaka. Book design by Ashim K. Biswas and produced by Abarton, 354 Dilu Road, Moghbazar. Printed at the Akota Offset Press, 119 Fakirapool, Dhaka, Bangladesh.

For Raina & Sumi

My backward place is where I am.
Nissim Ezekiel

Contents

**Published In The Streets Of Dhaka: Collected Poems
1966-2006 (2007)**

Poems (2002-2006)

From *The Gregorian* (1967)

From *Starting Lines* (Poems 1968-1975)

Poems in Subcontinental English

Black Orchid (1966)

Acknowledgements

Grateful acknowledgements are due to the editors of the following periodicals in which a number of these poems first appears: Acumen, The Cambridge Review, Chapman, Index on Censorship, Journal of Postcolonial Writing, Literature Matters, London Magazine, The Main Street Journal, Midland Poetry Worksheet, Poetry from Warwick University, Wasafiri (UK); Ariel (Canada); World Literature Written in English (Singapore); Alumni News (Department of English, University of Dhaka); The Daily Star, Form, New Age, Six Seasons Review, Spectrum, Bengal Lights: online (Bangladesh); Literature Alive, New Quest (India); The Asiatic (Malaysia); Drunken Boat: online, Brooklyn Voice: online, Catamaran (USA); Transnational Literature: online (Australia); Navasilu (Sri Lanka).

'Battambang' was commissioned by the Barbican Arts Centre, London.

A few poems have been anthologized in Stories from South Asia, John Welch, ed. (Oxford University Press, 1988); The Worlds of Muslim Imagination, Alamgir Hashmi, ed. (Islamabad, 1986); Imagine (Oslo); The Arnold Anthology of Post-Colonial Literatures, John Thieme, ed. (1996); Post-Independence Voices in South Asian Writings, M. Lal, A. Hashmi and V. Ramraj, eds. (Delhi, 2001); Immortal Words, Harihar Rath and A. J. Khan, eds. (Bhubaneswar, 2005); The Table is Laid: Anthology of South Asian Food Writings, John Thieme, ed. (Delhi: OUP, 2007); Masala, Debjani Chatterjee, ed. (London: Macmillan, 2005); Achiever's Course in English, for class VIII, Aloke Roy Chowdhury and Joyati Sen, eds. (Delhi: Orient Longman, 2006).

'An Anthology for Bangladeshi Poetry in English,' which is a sort of personal credo, first appeared in The Daily Star.

Thanks are due the Hawthornden Castle (Scotland) and Ledig House (USA) writers' colonies, and to the Poetry Café run by the Poetry Society, London, where I have been generously accommodated with residencies; and to the Royal Literary Fund which granted mea prized fellowship for a year at SOAS, London.

'Ode on the Lungi' has been recast and augmented several times since its first appearance in 2007, and has benefited from the comments and suggestions of kindly readers. It is a pleasure to acknowledge my debts in this regard, particularly to Rumana Siddique (who gifted the line 'One size fits all'), Sampurna Chatterji (who pointed out the kinship between lungi and dhoti), Mahbubur Rahman (who reminded me of the style of wearing a lungi while climbing trees) and Golam Kibria (who mentioned the use of the lungi as a carrying bag).

New Poems

Senior Citizen

I'm sixty.
Facetious fools say that's nothing
    if one's young at heart,
        or, absurdly: Sixty's the new forty.

Toeing them in the rump would give me a kick –
    only, a forty-year-old injury's
        come back to haunt the knee.

I'll just take things easy,
    let eyes wander where they will,
        forget to zip up after a pee,
    wear red underwear on Valentine's Day.

I wish mad old Nietzsche were right –
    wouldn't it be lovely
        living this unexceptional life
            over and over
            all eternity …

Liking It

It's the easiest thing to say
In the grey light of thinning hair:
I liked the world the way it was –
If only it had held steady
Time would be unchanging bliss!

What is it you so fondly remember
Amidst the glitches in recollection?
An album of snapshots,
Some video clips at best.
The mood that binds them together
Like an invisible rubber band
Comes out of a pocket you're wearing out now.

Maybe you can see
Clearer than your fast-fading fate line
An arched gate confettied with creepers
Golden green in early morning light,
Maybe your olfactories thrill
At the musky odor of blossoms
On a long-dead mango tree.

Or a remembered tale may set you
Dream-walking down village tracks
After a hurricane lantern swinging
Beneath a bullock cart's creaking chassis
Like a luminous pineapple…or scrotum.

But don't forget:
Calm cannot be retroactive.
The willed insouciance of youth
Crumpled before manic urgencies.
Why look back on such routine tussles?
Besides,
From the bottom of the well
One can only look up.

Not that a benign gaze answers:
The twinkling could be tinsel
And lights no superior tomorrow.
Better just carve a squiggle
On softening gray timber
At amber-gray dusk
And hum under your breath:
It's alright the way it is.

Playing Games

My little daughter has suddenly
        taken a fancy to board games –
ludo, draughts, snakes and ladders.
        And she insists we play with her.

The rules are beyond
        her comprehension though:
she just loves rattling the dice
        and moving the counters
any which way –

she's only playing at playing.
        And we play along,
charmed by the absurdity
        of it all,

and secure too
        in the knowledge
that before long
        she'll have the rules
at her fingertips

and we'll happily
        concede defeat
to her freshly acquired
        expertise.

There's a lesson here,
        for everything's a
game, as they say –
        war, love, work, politics,
what have you,

and from playing
        at playing a game

to actually playing it.
    one makes a full
quantum leap; it's what
    we call growing up:

if only we could be
    reasonably sure
our leaders
    would one day
stop playing at playing
    the game of democracy –
and start playing it.

Philosophy With Raina

Months short of six
Raina pauses
halfway through a glass of milk:

'Papa,
what do you get
if all the numbers
in the world
are put together?'

'Infinity.'

'How do you write it?'

'Like this...'

'Looks like an 8
put to sleep.'

'Why, yes, you're right.'

'Does it have *all*
the numbers?'

'Yes, I suppose.'

She goes back
to her milk
and Cartoon Network.

And now,
months short of seven,
she says,
'Papa,
I am thinking something.

You
are thinking something.
Mummy
is thinking something.
But I don't know
what you are thinking,
I don't know
what Mummy is thinking.
But why?'

How touching
that she thinks
Papa has the answer
to everything –
and how humbling.

Then she asks for
'a really scary
ghost story',
gets goose bumps listening
and goes to sleep snuggling
into her pillow.

Raina, you'll soon forget
you've asked these questions:
may they return
to tease your adult years
in those special moments
when you'll be alone with your thoughts
between life's cartoons
and scary ghost stories.

Pilgrims*

A translation of Rabindranath Tagore's *'Tirthajatri'*

In biting cold began our journey,
   A terribly long one too –
      And at the worst time imaginable,
The roads all circuitous,
   Winds sharp and blustery –
      An utterly impregnable winter.
The camels, with sore feet and chafed necks,
   Tetchily lie down in slush
      Sometimes our minds grow refractory
Recalling summer resorts in valleys,
   Their broad terraces, and young women in silk
      Serving sherbet. Our cameleers
Growl and curse and make off
   To look for women and booze.
      The torches sputter out
But there's no place to kip down,
   In towns and cities we are met
      With hostility or suspicion,
The villages are filthy, the prices they ask
   Outrageous: we are in for a hard time.
      At last we decide to travel all night,
Snatching a snooze now and then
   While a voice whispers in our ears –
      All this is sheer madness.

Towards dawn we came to a pleasantly cool valley
   Beneath the snow line, moist and heavy
      With the scent of dense vegetation.

---

* The Bengali poem by Rabindranath Tagore, 'Tirthajatri', collected in Punashcha, is itself a translation of T. S. Eliot's 'Journey of the Magi'. I thought the somewhat Borgesian exercise of translating the translation back into the language of the original, while carefully avoiding 'contamination' by the original poem itself, would amuse at least some readers.

A river sped along, the wheels of a mill
    Threshing the dark, and three trees
        Stood out against the horizon.
An ageing stallion galloped across the green.
    We came to an inn, by whose open vine-festooned door
        Two men sat dicing for high stakes,
Kicked away the empties of wine.
    But no one had any news,
        So we moved on, travelling till dusk.
The destined hour was nearly gone
    When we found the place –
        You might say it was most gratifying.

I remember, all this happened ages ago,
    Would that it happened again,
        But note this – please note this –
What was it drew us such a long way,
    Was it a quest for birth or death?
        Of course there was a birth,
No gainsaying that – we had proof incontrovertible.
    We had seen many a birth and death –
        And thought how different they were.
But this birth was hard to bear, sheer agony,
    Very like death, our own death.
        We came back, each to his homeland, his kingdom.
But we have lost all faith in the old order,
Amidst strange people clinging to their gods and goddesses.
    Another death would be most welcome.

Grishma, Barsha

The azan goes
round the city
in a rousing relay.

In the eastern sky
the grey of an old man's bottom
gives way to baby pink.

How about a conservatory
for muezzins?

Badshah Akbar had instructed
that the dawn azan
should be delivered
in Raga Ahir Bhairo –
it still is in Old Delhi,
a glorious aubade.

It's cool, it's warm, it's hot:
it's summertime.
The clock seems awry:
it's summer time
for the first time
here.
    Everything's late.
All the frogs in Rajasthan
married off –
         and still no rain.

The cattle all scrawny,
Krishna missing from Vrindavana.
Radha's prayer song's
a big hit –
         and still no rain.

Down in our sultry delta,
under a leaden sky,
I toss and turn and slip
into a sleep of hopelessness.

But the waking up's
miraculous –
the monsoon's upon us –
a month late –
and desperate
to make up
for lost time,

wind and water
playing furioso –

azan soaring
over rain clouds –

and Krishna's flute calling
Radha, Radha, Radha...

New Year Brainwave

(After rereading 'The Tempest')
for Ranjitda

'You give me fever' –
    Madonna on the iPod
        Pouring her heart out.

Nursing a common cold,
    I dwell on the
        Phenomenology of real fevers,

The mellow pleasures of
    The low-grade sort –
        Dry skin, mildly aching joints,

Mind disengaged from action –
    You could fancy yourself a Buddhist monk
        Or yogi in placid samadhi;

The irony of 'moderate' fever –
    You move from chill
        And tachycardia to stupor;

And high-grade fever that guarantees
    The high of delirium,
        After which comes hyperpyrexia –

And farewell life!
    Sipping hot tea in bed,
        I ride a New Year brainwave:

What if the peddlers of progress
    Could equip wielders of power
        With an efficient

Fever-inducing device?
    For writers, artists, intellectuals,
        Meditation-conducive 'low-grade',

No more than 39° C or 102.2° F,
    Should work wonders,
        And recalcitrant political activists

Could be taught instant moderation
    With moderate fever,
        39-40° C or 102.2-104° F.

Jails could be dismantled
    And criminals sentenced at home
        To a term of 'high-grade',

39-42° C or 104-107.6° F.
    For capital crimes it's higher still.
        The Global Mega-Power

With its Mega-Fever machines
    Could deal similarly with the whole world:
        Revive Oriental spiritual traditions

With a 'low-grade' pandemic, tame
    Rogue states with a mega-dose of 'moderate',
        Give terrorists a sharp taste of hyperpyrexia.

A perfect solution
    To mankind's ills,
        Don't you think? Utopia!

What are you saying?
    Product of a febrile imagination?
        So is every bleeding utopia, my friend.

On The Blink

My wall clock has stopped
With hour hand at 8
And minute hand at 36
Or 37, depending
On where you're looking from:
Parallax or something
I once learnt in high school science.
The second hand jerks
Between 40 and 41,
Like a discharging dick.

The batteries need changing
But I don't change them.
My wristwatch isn't on my wrist
But I don't open the drawer
To look at it
Or take it out and strap it on.
I've no idea what time it is
And I don't give a damn.

I don't turn on the radio or TV –
Keeps reminding you of the time.
The newspaper, slid under the door,
Takes a catnap – I glance at it
But don't pick it up
Or try to read the big headlines –
Feels good not to bother.
My head's light as a feather,
Without a care in the world –
A balloon filled with well-being.

The leaves on the trees
Play soft tambourine music –
So soft, it's only in my fancy I hear it.
The sun yawns and swallows

A procession of candyfloss clouds.
The day vanishes behind a veil of azure.
Feels like I could stay like this forever.
Don't know if I should put a word to it
But if you could ask Gautama
He'd perhaps tell you it's a kind of nirvana.

Ah, nirvana, I sigh,
Settling into the peace that passeth understanding,
And catch the prick hand bobbing
And then stop.
Just like that.
At once time rushes in
Through every crack and opening
With all the hideous clamour of voices and things,
Tales of time-serving technocrats,
Anxieties over time running out,
Promises revised and deferred,
The globe spinning out of control,
The 'Hidden Hunger'* of the headlines
And hosts of half-hidden desires –
The usual, nothing extraordinary –
For money, sex, power.
I take out my watch,
Start rummaging in the drawer
For a couple of double-A batteries.

---

* 'Hidden Hunger': Recently, during the military-backed caretaker government's tenure, 2007-2009, when it was alleged that rapid price rises had brought on famine in parts of Bangladesh, a government spokesman declared that that wasn't the case, there was only some 'hidden hunger'.

Six Shared Seasons

for Rubana, a true Southasian

Since we are
    our worst enemies,
        is it any surprise

that barbed wire,
    watchtower and searchlight
        keep neighbours apart,

border guards suddenly
    slug it out
        for no apparent reason,

families picnic
    willy-nilly, as they wait
        in visa queues,

and poor people are
    rounded up – undesirables
        or aliens or both –

we're almost as bad
    as Europe was
        till the other day.

All the time
    the year keeps rolling
        to its celestial schedule.

grishma's furnace heat,
    barsha, monsoon floods,
        sarat's mellow skies,

hemanta's fresh harvest,
    mist over the fields,
        dew underfoot,

warmth of embroidered quilts,
 winter bonfires, snow on mountains,
  fog on the plains,

then every girl a beauty
 in *basanta's* vibrant amber,
  & flowers with humid lips

kissing the passionate bee.
 Six seasons to everyone else's
  four – from the Himalayas

to Serendip, & the Indus plains
 to the delta
  of the Ganges & Brahmaputra –

hold the whole
 of Southasia* together,
  six shared seasons

making nought
 of borders & barbed wire.
  Nature as usual, is

prodigal with gifts and lessons –
 & as usual, alas,
  we take one & ignore the other.

---

* Writing 'Southasia' instead of 'South Asia' is a charming orthographic innovation that indicates the region's civilizational unity; it is used by *Himal*, the magazine published from Kathmandu, and the Southasian TV Channel, of which Rubana was CEO for some years.

Poor Man Eating

Were I a painter
I am sure
My signature theme would be
The title of this poem.

The sun races to the zenith,
Imperious as an oriental autocrat.
The poor man crouches
In imitation Tommy Hilfiger rags
In the dwindling shade
Of a denuded tree.

His hands cradle
A bowl of fired earth –
It could be an Ouija board
To conjure up goodies,
Courtesy of the weak of conscience.

And when they come,
How he falls to it!
Eyes focused in mystic concentration,
Left arm protectively around
The pile of comestibles,
As right hand shovels them
Into an eager mouth.

I would paint the scene
Over and over
In luscious oil:
The painted proliferation
Might work magic,
Converting seeming impossibility
Into palpable reality:

All the world's poor
Men and women

Gathered as if on the mythic day
Of final reckoning,
On this lowly earth,
Devouring earthly fare:
O the gods would come down
To bless and share!

All Is Well

(Derived From The Film Three Idiots, And Dedicated To Its Cast)

Our blind nightwatchman
rises from a postprandial nap
at midnight
and starts on his rounds
through familiar lanes and alleyways
with their familiar smells
and resident pack of loud-
mouthed strays,
strikes the familiar lamp-posts
with his old cane staff
and lets out the familiar
reassuring cry…

Not that thieves and burglars
are kept entirely at bay,
but the incidence of their success
is the same,
roughly,
as the national average.

And though strangers
hearing of him
burst out laughing,
we'd prefer him
to anything else,
even Blackwater, Inc.
We wouldn't be able to sleep at all
if we didn't hear his outlandish
drawled
barely intelligible
demotic English cry –
'Olleej Oil! Olleej oil!…'
All is well! All is well! –
in this poor neighbourhood
where everyone speaks
demotic Bengali.

Trees
A Prose Poem

Surely you've noticed how, as soon as you get out of the city, the sight of trees and greenery lifts up the spirits, even to the point of elation. The reason for this, I'm certain, has to do with evolutionary psychology. Our mind is essentially the same as that of our earliest ancestors on the African savanna, where foliage meant food – to pluck or trap or hunt. Plants and trees and grassland, so to speak, meant both nature and nurture.

I wonder if our evolutionary connection with vegetation goes deeper still. Is it too fanciful to imagine that trees inspired our evolution into two-legged homo sapiens sapiens? I can see our almost-human predecessors staring awe-struck at the vertical rise of tree-trunks, topped by varied and quite fantastic hairstyles, and then pushing off the earth with their forefeet in an attempt to stand shoulder to shoulder with them. Needless to say, those who succeed reach out with their hands to pluck the appetizing fruit nestling amidst the boughs. The rest is Darwinian commonsense.

Later, when mankind had found their best friend in the dog, the dutiful canine quadruped, like an ideal slave, identified completely with the master, to the extent of trying to emulate the tree-like stance. Alas, it could only manage to make a tripod of itself. The poor creature's frustration and resentment settled into a subliminal layer of its psyche – to obtain pleasing release each time it raised a rear leg to deluge the roots of a tree.

Dear Sir*

Dear Sir,
How well we remember
That season of fond hopes
And imperious desires,
The salt breeze of a sure future
Navigating through the maze
Of this old city's streets and lanes
To nudge us in warm intimacy.

Between the adrenalin rush
Of the protest march
And the quiet delights
Of classroom theatre
We split our serious hours
And still saved a few
To waste as we wished.

What did we gather
As we foregathered
For early morning lectures
And mid-morning tutorials?
Wisdom, knowledge or information?
Did it entirely depend
On one's interpretive bent?

Or was it a style
And not just content,
Matter and manner
Inseparably blent?
Not soap but classic opera?
Above the demagogic baritones
Your tentative tenor still rose

* This poem was originally written for a festschrift in honour of Professor Khan Sarwar Murshid.

To fastidiously reiterate:
Even when inexorable blight
Taints the world at large
There is room in the heart
For 'sweetness and light'.

Is that what drew some of us
To follow you into the peculiar
Profession of professing letters?
But first we had to face
The palindromic chatter
Of carbine and machine-gun fire
And be reborn in the giddy air
Of freedom and its discontents.

We woke up one fine morning
To find the Groves of Academe globalized
Into a downmarket shopping mall
Trading briskly in various degrees
Of proven value on the job market.
Pushing literature I am cast
In the role of the 'farcical pedagogue'
Once played by Stephen Daedalus.
The younger generation show
No taste for 'sweetness and light'.
In a world of texting and email
Letters are of no avail.

We are both old-fashioned then,
Making nought of the notorious
Gap between one generation
And the next. It's time for us
To make a stand, affirming
The worth of things we cherish.
Age is no matter, Man doesn't grow
Old – the world grows old,
It's sinking beneath our feet,

Let it sink – our task is to think
And sing of our true heritage.

To conclude I should like to go back
To the style of a more ceremonious age
And declare that I remain
Your most obedient pupil,

                                    Kaiser Haq

Ode On The Lungi

for Shawkat and Baby Osman

Grandpa Walt,
allow me to share
my thoughts with you

if only because
every time I read

'Passage to India'
and come across

the phrase
'passage to more than India'
I fancy,

anachronistically,
that you wanted
to overshoot the target

by a shadow line
and land in Bangladesh.

Lately, I've been thinking a lot
about sartorial equality.

How far we are from
this democratic ideal!

And how hypocritical!
'All clothes have equal rights' –
this nobody will deny

and yet, some obviously
are more equal than others.

No, I'm not complaining about
the jacket and tie
required in certain places –

that, like fancy dress parties,
is in the spirit of a game.

I'm talking of
something more fundamental.

Hundreds of millions
of men and women,

from the Pacific to Africa
wear the lungi,

also known variously
as the sarong, munda, htamain, saaram,

pinon, ma'awaiis, kitenge, kanga, kaiki,
or the variant dhoti.

They wear it day in day out,
indoors and out.

Just think –
at any one moment

there are more people in lungis
than the population
of Europe and the USA.

Now try wearing one
to a White House appointment –

not even you, Grandpa Walt,
laureate of democracy,
will make it in.

You would if you
affected a kilt –
but a lungi? No way.

But why? – this is the question
I ask all to ponder.

Is it a clash of civilizations?
The sheer absurdity of it –

the kilt is with 'us'
but the lungi is with 'them'!

Think too of neo-imperialism
and sartorial hegemony,

how brown and yellow sahibs
in natty suits
crinkle their noses

at compatriots
(even close relations)
in modest lungis:

exceptions only prove the rule,
Sri Lanka, for instance, where
colourful sarongs are party wear,

or Myanmar
where political honchos
queue up in lungis
to receive visiting dignitaries.

But then, Myanmar dozes
behind a cane curtain,
a half pariah among nations.

Wait till it's globalised:
Savile Row will acquire
a fresh crop of patrons.

Hegemony invades private space
as well: my cousin in America

would get home from work
and lounge in a lungi –

till his son grew ashamed
of dad and started hiding
the 'ridiculous ethnic attire'.

It's all too depressing.
But I won't leave it at that.

The situation is desperate.
Something needs to be done.

I've decided not to
take it lying down.

The next time someone insinuates
that I live in an Ivory Tower

I'll proudly proclaim
I AM A LUNGI ACTIVIST!

Friends and fellow lungi lovers,
let us organize lungi parties and lungi parades,

let us lobby Hallmark and Archies
to introduce an international Lungi Day

when the UN Chief will wear a lungi
and address the world.
Grandpa Walt, I celebrate my lungi
and sing my lungi

and what I wear
you shall wear.

It's time you finally made your passage
to more than India – to Bangladesh –

and lounging in a lungi
in a cottage on Cox's Bazar beach

(the longest in the world, we proudly claim)
watched 28 young men in lungis bathing in the sea.

But what is this *thing*
(my learned friends,
I'm alluding to Beau Brummell),

I repeat, what is this thing
I'm going on about?

A rectangular cloth,
white, coloured, check or plaid,

roughly 45X80 inches,
halved lengthwise

and stitched
to make a tube

you can get into
and fasten in a slipknot

around the waist –
One size fits all!

And should you pick up dirt
say on your seat
you can simply turn it inside out.

The hem serves as napkin
to wipe the hands

or mouth after a rinse,
taking a deep bow

to bring lips to raised
lungi edge: only ensure

it's not raised too high,
especially if you aren't
wearing underwear.

When you are out of it
the lungi can be folded up
like a scarf.

Worn out, it has its uses –
as dish rag or floor wipe
or material for a *kantha* quilt.

Or you can let your imagination
play with the textile tube

to illustrate the superstrings
of the 'Theory of Everything'

(vide, the book of this title
by the venerable Stephen Hawking).

Coming back to basics,
the lungi is an elaborate fig-leaf,

the foundation of propriety
in ordinary mortals.

Most of the year, when barebodied
is cool, you can lead a decent life
with only a couple of lungis,

dipping in pond or river
or swimming in a lungi

abbreviated into a G-string,
then changing into the other one.

Under the hot sun
a lungi can become

Arab-style headgear
or Sikh-style turban.

Come chilly weather
the spare lungi can be
an improvised poncho.

The lungi as G-string
can be worn to wrestle
or play kabaddi

but on football or cricket field
or wading through the monsoon

it's folded vertically
and kilted at the knee.

In short
the lungi is a complete wardrobe
for anyone interested;

an emblem of egalitarianism,
symbol of global left-outs.

Raised and flapped amidst laughter
it's the subaltern speaking.

The lungi undoubtedly
is the most wanker-friendly garment.
If you are bothered by random erections

you can discreetly inveigle your hand
from above or below
even in polite company

and while insouciantly carrying on
a conversation on the deconstruction
of metaphysics,

just do the needful. And more:
when romance strikes, the lungi
is a sleeping bag for two:

a book of smutty jokes, a bottle of hooch
and your beloved inside your lungi –
there's paradise for you.

If your luck runs out
and the monsoon turns into
a biblical deluge

just get in the water
and hand-pump air

to balloon up your lungi –
now your humble ark.

When you find shelter
on a treetop
take it off,

rinse it,
hold it aloft –

flag of your indisposition –
and wave it at the useless stars!

East And West
A Plan for World Peace

East is East and West is West, and never the twain shall meet.
                                        – *Rudyard Kipling*

Holy the rumblings in my gut! holy my shit in the toilet!
                                        – *Allen Ginsberg*

Thanks to Uncle Freud we know
How seemingly trivial things like jokes
Or a slip of the tongue
Can open a trapdoor
To the turgid depths of the Unconscious,
Its unsuspected eddies
        and cross
                and countercurrents.

Other little things too,
        I dare say,
Are loaded with
        (hidden) meaning...
Umm...take for instance
                styles of cleanliness
Which, it's said,
        is next to godliness –
Enough to tell you
        there's more to it
                than meets the eye.

Consider the ways we clean genitals or bottoms,
See how culture locks us into intractable difference.
You could sum it up in a smart soundbite:
                EAST IS WASH,
                        WEST IS WIPE!

True,
        and yet,
                like all binary oppositions,

35

Readily deconstructed.
The Chinese are wipers,
Their ancient forebears in fact
                invented toilet paper!
The French on the other hand
Invented the bidet –
                one reason why
Anglo-Saxons consider them rather peculiar!
Ancient Romans used a stick
Attached to sponge and soaked in brine –
                something like a modern toilet cleaner.
Before toilet paper in the West
Rags, straw, leaves, what have you,
Or, as Dryden's 'MacFlecknoe' reminds us,
Remaindered books; and across
The Atlantic, the Sears Catalogue
Came in handy for a wipe.
Eskimos used snow or tundra grass,
Arabs sand and pebbles.
And the Maori, Hottentot, Amerindians and all
Our other cousins
                packed tight into this topsy-turvy planet?
Scope for serious research here
And interventions for the cause of world peace!
Let us break down silly prejudice!

A friend got into an argument with a Westerner.
'How,' said one, 'can you bear to touch
Your unclean bum with your hand?'
'And how can you,' the other came back,
'Leave a layer of shit on yours?'
Gentlemen! Gentlemen! one would feel like interjecting,
It's terrible that we don't revere
Each other's gods – let us at least
Respect each other's bottoms!
In the ways we clean up
There's variety to rejoice over – not cavil –

36

And even lessons in philosophy:
Check it out if you don't
Believe me – it's on the net:
60% of Westerners
Wipe back to front
And take a good look at the soiled paper
Before dropping it in the bowl –
Isn't it piquant homage
To the Socratic injunction
Know Thyself?

Let us therefore give the matter due attention,
Let us organize televised toilet festivals
Where UN ambassadors from every nation
Will discuss and demonstrate varied means
Of washing and wiping.
      Let 5-star hotels
And holiday resorts
    offer a sampling of exotic toilets:
Igloo toilets dispensing snow and tundra grass,
Desert tent toilets with sand and pebbles,
Elizabethan toilets equipped with rags,
Augustan toilets with first editions of Thomas Shadwell,
American ones with 19th century Sears catalogues,
Roman toilets where guests in togas
Apply a saline sponge-tipped stick,
South Asian toilets where guests in lungi or dhoti
    pour water out of lota or bodna
        as they wash.

Already,
    we can proudly report,
The nations have been drawing closer
    to each other's toilet habits –
Every corner shop here is well-stocked
    with toilet rolls,
And judging by testimony on the net
    Westerners seem happy

Directing a jet of water bottomwards
    from an innovative nozzle
Before they wipe –
    all without encouragement
From government or international agencies.

A little concerted effort
    to further the process
And we'll have a better world by far.
    And so,
Let world leaders gathering
    to talk peace
Generate mutual goodwill
    by cleaning each other's bottoms!
Should they still
    grumble and growl
Mahatma Gandhi from high heaven
    will pipe in:
        'Stop all this hungamma!
        Come and have an enema!'

Published In The Streets Of Dhaka: Collected Poems
1966-2006

Poems (2002-2006)

Windows

'Look!
These buildings are like ghost ships
In the gathering dark.'

      'Yes, but look again,
      The lights have come on,
      There are people moving around.'

'But they look so remote, so alien,
The figures in the windows
Just like cardboard cutouts.'

      'True, and yet,
      Dearest, those oblongs of light
      Are our home...'

...Fragile slates
On which we may adumbrate
Our unsteady kisses.'

Figures Of Speech

It pleases me greatly that my ancestral village stands on a
river
if only because running water lends itself to profound
observations
e.g. Heraclitus's aphorism about the impossibility
of stepping into the same river twice
which I revise in the light of Lord Buddha's wisdom, viz.
it isn't quite the same person who steps in the second time
& suddenly for no rhyme or reason remembering
Rimbaud's mysterious self-definition
Je est un autre
see
clear as the dear cool water
a small boy thrill to the liquid touch
as it laves around skinny shanks
& leaves mica glitters on dark skin
while a slippery susu in the distance
punctuates the rippling syllables – a kinetic comma! –
& small fishing boats fill up with a rainbow-bright catch.

Now cut to the present: peer into the constricted river's
polluted mirror,
watch your haunted eyes tremble:
no flash of fin excites the shallows,
the water's unfit to drink,
unfit to swim in,
unfit to touch...

Looking over this depressing draft for a poem
only the images seem to have any life,
similes and metaphors as sharp and clear
as the river is murky –
                    that's another one;
well, as doom
            looms – nice sound effect there

eh? anyway –
         as doom
looms –
         you might of course interject
that it always does –
         still, right now
as our very own
         doom
             looms
is that all we have
         to fall back on –
             figures of speech?

Weltanschauung

... the author's style is directly bound up with a conception of the world; the sentence and paragraph structure, the use and position of the substantive, the verb, etc., the arrangement of the paragraphs, and the qualities of the narrative – to refer to only a few specific points – all express hidden presuppositions ....

–Jean-Paul Sartre, *The Problem of Method*

Quite true, *Maitre,*
    though you've forgotten
        to mention

punctuation –
    that too matters
        just as much:

an author's favourite mark
    tells you something crucial
        about her *Weltanschauung*

especially in this new
    e-mail-mad millennium . . .
        Mine, I can tell you

at once, is neither
    comma, colon (full or semi),
        full stop, dash,

exclamation
    or interrogation
        mark, but the hybrid

interrobang,
    which needs no text
        & can stand

in mocking autonomy,
    a complete critique
        of the passing show.

Spend, Spending, Spent

How do I spend my days?
Late nights and rising late,
distracted by celestial lights,
meaning sun, moon, star,
nature's changes of fashion,
overdressed summer, nudist winter,
lingual monotony of fellow creatures,
shrilling kite, shrieking parrot, rasping crow,
lazing till hunger overwhelms, then
eating without relish,
scanning violent headlines
while straining to overcome constipation,
breaking into nervous sweat
as clock hands admonish
my tardiness,
and yet somehow managing
to get clothes on, get through
the day, the murderous decibels
of hucksters, honkers, sloganeers,
and seized with sudden enthusiasm
for health and strength and vigour
once again attack a pair of
rusty dumb-bells –
            but they seem heavier
each time I get down to it.
            Well, it seems
I no longer spend
my days,
            they
spend me.

Monsoon Poem With Prose Postscript

Even large print blurs
        in draining light.
One could imagine Purgatory –
        a vast shanty town –
set ablaze, smoke
        becoming ink-black clouds,
setting the mood
        for monsoon's advent.

Find yourself a bamboo hut –
        mud floor, tin roof –
and wait as moist air wraps
you like a winding sheet.

It comes:
        a drop
on the tin roof –
        C sharp!

And more,
        beating a tattoo,
pounding dust
        to release a roar;
it seems the ground beneath
        might dissolve
like sugar cubes in tea.

Buddha says: *Everything is transient; clutch at nothing – and his disciples holed up in monasteries to meditate on his teaching till the rains let up. I would like to meditate too but I have to go to a party – where the inane chatter on the monsoon's beauty – unique to our land – and Rabindranath Tagore's divine lyrics on the theme is enough to drive me nuts. My monsoon thoughts are now of noxious gutters swelling into a deluge, carrying away the detritus of all our days.*

Truth On The Prowl

Browsing through Vedantic verdure
He reads: *The Truth is one
And indivisible...*
It lulls him to sleep.

He dreams:
Truth is single
And lonely:
On the prowl.

But everyone keeps away.
Truth goes to Singles Bars
But no one's interested –
Neither men nor women,
Straight, gay, lesbian, bi.

Finally Truth meets Falsity,
Fixes a date –
                and is stood up.

Truth looks into a mirror,
Touches itself –
                nothing happens.

Truth sits alone
Drinking, lugubriously
Watches men and women
Busy at their pleasures.

Dateline, Dhaka, 25 March 2006*
(*To my fellow Freedom Fighters*)

Silken afternoon light
Slips through the fingers
Of minute hands
As wind-up clocks
Clear their throats
And spit out the hour.

A wistful shadow
Clouds our eyes:
Swiftly gathering dusk
Suggests linked hands
And stolen kisses;

No such luck for us:
Cynical romantics
Pretending insouciance,
Talking realpolitik,
And – let's face it –
Regular wankers.

After the usual
Overfried comestibles,
Sick jokes, syrupy tea,
Round of three-card poker
And cigarettes, cigarettes, cigarettes,

Who'd have thought
We'd be waylaid
By History –
Sounds portentous
But how else to put it?

---

* The Bangladesh independence war started after the Pakistan Army's bloody crackdown on civilians on 25 March 1971.

As we picked our way
Around improvised barricades
To reach home under exploding skies,
Amidst slain bodies
The ultimate choice –
Fight or flee –
Fixed us in a gorgon stare.

We stared back, unpetrified
(Though scared) and vowed
To fight till all were free.
It was precisely
Half a biblical lifetime ago
Though on this day once again
It feels like it was yesterday.

A To Z, Azad

*for Humayun Azad**

Something is dying in us
and we watch in bewilderment;

it was perhaps the best thing
in us, and with all our niggling flaws
marked us still as human:

we thought the world
or at least our corner of it
could be made
if not better
    at least less bad,

but it's only getting worse –
looks like we've been had.
True, we won a war –
or at least a Victory Day
but more than what we won's
at stake in battles that rage
around us every day.
               When
To live and let live
is a philosophy
minced with butcher's knives
the thinking mind must reiterate
before the powers that be
and the powers that are desperate
to be the powers that be
some simple lessons of civilization:

---

* Professor Humayun Azad, who wrote a scathing satire on Islamic militants, was brutally attacked on 27 February 2004 as he was leaving a book fair. He survived, almost miraculously, but died of a heart attack a few months later. The poem was written within days of the attack.

Ballot-box democracy is meaningless
without nomocracy (please
look it up
in a dictionary –
you need a big one for this,
I'm afraid)

To say there is no world
but what we make with words
and what we call truth
is only a construct
may be delectable
postmodern fashion
for academic consumption
but to make untruth with words
is nothing but to lie

And to drag God's name down
into the gutter of politics
is utterly flagitious
or monstrously insane

To be *azad*, to be free
to walk, talk, write, sing,
love, draw, dance
is the A to Z of life,
the rest is death
     death
     death
     death
     death

I could go on and on
but why be schoolmasterly?
I could take a cue from René Magritte
and write:
despite the hint of metre

and the desultory rhyme
Ceci n'est pas un poeme –
                    instead
I'll adapt some words
from sombre Wilfrid Owen,
killed on the Sambre Canal,
whose spirit still haunts the literate:

I am not concerned here with Poetry.
My subject is Life, and the protest
against the enemies of Life.
The Poetry is in the Protest.

Battambang

Out of this tangle of texts and things and beings
she springs up like a weed –
                              uprooted, cast
to the winds, propelled
by hunger through flat spaces, across fetid swamps,
rivers porridge-thick after the rains,
towards the straight line of sky
and earth meeting edge to edge,
towards hills and valleys with romantic names,
eating young rice shoots, begging for bones,
stealing salted fish
                    (secreted between scraggy breasts),
always where she halts
someone turns up to shoo her away.

Sometimes, if a man following her about
asks her name, where she is from,
in a language she scarce understands,
all she says is, 'Battambang.'

One, two, three....she'd count the days
out of home. Now, all sense of time
(or numbers) gone, she only knows a gnawing inside
as her belly, infected with life, rises like dough
stretching skin till it cracks.
(It's only to die quietly that the child is born.)

Hair, pulled in despair, comes off in clumps
leaving her looking like a grubby Buddhist nun.
Lying in a gravel pit she gazes mesmerised
at distant stars, nearby town lights
where thousands like her huddle in corridors of wind.
In dreams she turns into her dead child
walking through mountains and city walls.

Ten years from home, she comes upon ragged millions
thronging the Jessore Road towards Calcutta.
Air like the inside of a rotten egg: monsoon.
The tortured city smells of sweat, saffron, stagnant water.
Perhaps our paths crossed: hers and a burly, bearded poet's
and mine, as I headed for a theatre of war. They say
she once pulled a live fish from between her breasts
and with delirious shrieks bit off its head,
but on party nights devoured
foie gras sandwiches from embassy bins.

The war ended. Like women dancing in a trance
to shake off the spirits of war-dead spouses
I chucked half a life into the bin

till,
one clear autumn morning I see her –
it can only be her, with her crazy eyes, her tatty sarong –
by the overflowing skip in front of the British
Council in Dhaka, boiling rice in a battered pan.
The scent spreads as vapour rises skyward
and she bursts into song –
a joyous song of Battambang.

London, 2003.

This poem was commissioned by the Barbican Arts Centre, for a series of readings to accompany an exhibition of photographs of migrants, refugees and other displaced persons taken by the Brazilian economist Sebastiao Salgado. Looking at these photographs I realized that behind each of them lay a tale of great existential significance. The significance could be sensed, perhaps as an aura, though the tale itself might be irrecoverable beyond the bland details of a news report. However, my experience of the 1971 Bangladesh war of independence fused with the nightmarish tale of the madwoman from Indo-China in Marguerite Duras' novel 'The Vice-Consul', to provide me with a miniature narrative and a set of powerful images that reflect the extreme situation of so many of Salgado's displaced persons.

Duras' anonymous character utters only one word in the novel, the name of her native village: Battambang. For me this awkward-sounding name symbolizes the home all exiles have left behind, as well as the home they seek to create for themselves wherever they have fetched up: this explains the title of my poem.

The burly, bearded poet is Allen Ginsberg, who came to India in 1971 and wrote a poem titled, 'September on Jessore Road.' Needless to say, the identification of Duras' madwoman with a madwoman who used to haunt the corner of Dhaka where I live is purely fanciful.

New Year Bagatelle*

A fine time
we are having
when a year passes away
unwaked
and a new one slips in
untoasted

My hi-tech toy
livens things up a bit:
a friend's picture SMS
sighs: Adieu
2005,
the integers flanking
a nude female torso
whose breasts double
as noughts –

and O O O
what noughts,
the infinite being
of their circularity
(if I may be permitted
a mathematico-
metaphysical shuffle)
a pert rebuff
to sartorial fascism
Or could they be
a grimly humorous warning –
stylized bombs
with detonator nipples?
Well, you can have
your semiotic pick
as irreversible days unravel
their own slippery tale

---

* At the turn of 2005 public celebrations on New Year's eve were officially
forbidden in Dhaka in order to preempt rowdyism.

Bloomsday Centenary Poem
In Free Verse And Prose

16 June 2004 –
         Imagine!
A hundred years
since Stephen Dedalus and Leopold
(Poldy) Bloom stepped out
of their respective homes
in Dublin ... fair city
where girls are so pretty ...

Imagine the day
in another city (town rather)
with the same initial –
         Dhaka.

Let
two of its denizens,
separated
     like the Hibernian anti-heroes,
by age and religious heritage
enact the Odyssean perambulations
through fetid, waterlogged lanes,
clutching dripping umbrellas –
the monsoon having arrived
     with a bang –
and tiptoeing through slush.
Their names ... one must have
     a mythic ring ...

how about Ali Baba Sindbad,
     and the other, stolidly resonant ...

Babu Hurree Chunder Mookherjee,
     that extraordinary creation
of the master of Anglo-Indian fusion,
     Ruddy Yaar Kiplingam –
you know who I mean.

As for correspondence between chapters, why, 'Circe' is of course set in the old red light district of Kandu Patti; 'Scylla and Charybdis' in the Northbrook Hall Library: the subject of the impassioned debate that takes place there isn't about Shakespeare's supposed cuckoldry, as in the Dublin version, but something equally exciting, whether 'tis nobler to pursue Vaishnavite devotion with the help of one's own spouse or someone else's. For the rest, let undergrads toil on it as a tutorial assignment, meticulously plotting Joyce's Dublin on to our tropical metropolis.

Suddenly
      I am struck
By a double-barrelled epiphany:
Dublin is Dhaka is any city
And Bloomsday is today is any day ...

Henceforth,
      The map of Dublin as in Ulysses,
Suffices for all cities,
And calendars are redundant
      For everyday in Bloomsday ...

Hurree Babu (for you are perennial citizen of these sultry parts), kindly note: here's a suitable topic for yet another of your submissions to *Notes & Queries*, even though to be only rejected, like the others to the Royal Society, and eventually to be included in a privately printed limited edition of a definitive collection of all your unpublished adumbrations.

Dhaka, Bloomsday, 2004

Lord Of A Dark Sun

(A poem in commemoration of Rabindranath Tagore's birthday)

What's in a name?

There can be a lot
    in a name.
Take one that means

Lord of the Sun:
    can you dismiss it
as easily as
    just plain Rose?
And should its bearer
    conceal it behind
a comic synonym
    as you did,
Grandfather-Poet,
    the farcical comeuppance
is well-deserved:
    a doctoral thesis
of Teutonic solemnity
    on a fictive author!
Of course you relished the joke
    as much as anyone –
your second nature's childlike play,
    much as your vassal
in the sky plays hide and seek
    with clouds, charming
mortal eyes with celestial chiaroscuro.

For every sad and sweet
    nuance of feeling
you have a song and dance routine.
    If that's snide
let me be blunt:
    too often your prose
reads like Madame Blavatsky.

Let provincial culture-vultures
    and New Age pseud-
o cosmopolitans keep
    you in those aspects.
But when our blighted age
    catches up with ... er ...
your perennial philosophy,
    turning your pen
into a tormented artist's tool,
    when you wield words
like scimitars that slice
    through the herd's holy cows,
you remain an exemplar
    for our entropic millennium,
Lord of the Sun,
Lord of a Dark Sun.

The Waistline

(with due apologies to the spirit of T. S. Eliot)

Corsets are the cruellest things –
breathing's impossible
and the mammaries
crowded painfully together;
it was so lovely to lie
in bed with nothing on:
but that's the price you have to pay
for a sleek waistline
that sets men drooling.
Somers surprised me, as I came
out of the bungalow, and suggested
a drive; he's a distant cousin,
Superintendent of Police in Dacca
in this year of the Lord 1888,
and an arch-puke, always getting drunk
and throwing up, but a handsome devil
nonetheless.
            Karim Khan, his Pathan sais,
a baroque-moustached giant
with a thing for boys, I'm told,
set the horses careening towards Ramna.
'Ghoomtay raho,' shouted Somers
when we got there, & I knew
he had something on his mind.
'I had a Bengali babu teach me
a few words,' he said. 'Like what?'
I asked. 'Ami tomay bhalobashi,'
he said. 'And what's that?'
I asked, feigning ignorance,
'I love you,' he said. I could hear
him breathing hard. 'Oh,' I said,
feigning nonchalance, as I looked
out the window, my waistline stretched
like a sharp knife. 'Will you marry me?'

61

he asked, hoarse with excitement,
and grabbed me by the waist.
Then round and round Ramna
we went, as in that filthy French novel
I read in finishing school after lights out –
Madame Bovary. He said, Mary,
Mary, hold on tight, I'm coming.
And how he did! But doing it in the carriage
felt so cheap.
         And now he's gone,
eloped with Jenny Maltravers,
the Jailor's niece. Always knew
he was a rotter. I'm growing bigger
every day. It's not so much
the scandal I mind but that,
corset or no corset,
for a whole year it's farewell
waistline! I read,
much of the night, and will soon
get down to writing a novel
sizzling with sex, set in the sultry East.

Two Paradies

ms bunny sen
*(with due apologies to the spirits of jibanananda das, e. e. lower
case cummings & t. s. eliot)*

been buggering around this goddamn city
for godknowshowlong –
feels like a thousand bloody years,
    no kidding;
from bongshal's rancid restaurants
to gulshan's toxic lake
I've trod every effing inch
& on pitch-dark nights
of power outages as well.
i've been in burra kuttra
in grey twilight
& in distant rayerbazar
in moonless dark,
& all for what
i ask you –
a few bloody takas
for which i have to shout
myself hoarse
tutoring the unteachable
scions of nouveau riche swine
swimming in champagne bubbles,
i feel absobloodylutely
knackered, i tell you,
just couldn't go on
if it weren't for a few moments
with ms bunny sen
of banglamotor.

o her hair is like the dark sky
above sangsad bhaban
& her face is just

like aishwariya's.
imagine a sailor
adrift on a wreck
suddenly coming upon
a green island
smelling of rich spices –
that's how i felt when she came
and sat across the table
in a dimly-lit fast food joint,
spreading the musky scent
of allure (from chanel);
whatsup? she said
raising those gorgeously
made-up eyes
like exotic bird's nests –
i could just curl up
inside them
and happily
die.

when day goes kaput
the dark sneaks in
like silent dew;
buzzards wipe the smell
of sun off filthy wings;
colour seeps out of everything.
in faraway hamlets
glowing fireflies announce
it's storytelling hour;
time to take pen and paper
out of the jammed drawer
& do my daily
creative writing act –
tho' godaloneknows
to what bloody end.
the birds come home to roost,
the bleeding rivers end where they began,

life's wheeling & dealing
can't go on forever; it's all
dark, dark, dark
but for the tête-à-tête
with ms bunny sen of banglarnotor.

Three Minimalist Poems In Monosyllabic
Vers Libre

1. A Minimalist Credo

less
is
more

more
or
less

2. Snapshot

Say
Cheese!

But
your
smile
is
cool

as
a
frog's
arse

3. Illumination/Nirvana

You
see
the
light

and
at
once

start
to
live

here
&
now

The Raven

(On the fortieth birthday of the Canadian poet Eleonore Schönmeier)

Once again the monsoon's here,
furious with wind and water
deluging verdure, sweeping away
telephone poles, wireless installations,
paralysing computers, seeping into mailbags,
even incapacitating trusty old carrier pigeons
with a strange new virus that – who knows –
might have been created in a distant lab
and let loose to disrupt communication
between individuals of an unusual sort …

Well, anyway, what the hell to do?
Not being metaphysical enough
to trust in telepathy
I turn the pages of the Edgar Allan Poe catalogue –
the choice is predictable enough –
& turn instantly into a raven,
albeit a monsoon-bedraggled one
          with a ten-thousand-mile flight ahead …

Across entropic cities, polluted seas,
surreal landscapes, flapping
ungainly wings, devouring garbage
I'll yet make a timely landfall
& upon the blessed midnight when
the radiant lady whom the angels named Eleonore
turns forty – & not a day more –
gently rap, rap at her chamber door
& croak, though weary, quite distinctly,
'I come from the opposite corner
of this desolate earth to bring such greetings
& love as only friends can bring to each other,'
& should she ask 'Will you always be a friend?'
address with all my remaining strength
a single word to the gentle Eleonore: 'FOREVERMORE!'

A Rationale For Criticism

'Everything,'
    said Mallarme,
'exists
    to end up
in a book.'

'Quite,'
    says the critic –
'even
    a book.'

As Usual

As usual
My old friend
The Sage of the Roadside Tea-stall
Casually solves a problem or two
Between sips of semi-viscous tea
For which, as usual, I am paying
Because, as usual, he is out of pocket.

The talk, as usual, is of money –
Ministers and their multi-millions,
Captains of commerce and their borrowed billions,
Spiralling prices and dwindling incomes.

'Ban money,' the Sage counsels.
'Abolish currency, and peace
Will reign on earth.'
Silence descends upon us
Like feathers from ruffled chickens.

All eyes are trained on the Sage
Imploring elaboration. 'No money –
No desire for money, no pickpocketing,
No bribes, no violence;
No taka – no trickery,
No pounds sterling – no pound of flesh,
No moolah – no murder,
No greenbacks – no Green Berets.'

The Sage pauses,
Takes a long sip
And a sagacious conceptual leap:
'I am of course using the word money
In a broadly symbolic sense.
By money I mean everything
That arouses cupidity –

Gold, diamonds, cars...
I mean, in fact,
Private property.'

'What about power?' I ask.
(You see, I've read my Michel Foucault.)
'I was coming to that,'
Says the wily Sage.
'Abolish power as well.
No more power play
Between politicians and the people,
Between teachers and the taught,
Between friends, lovers, relatives,
Family members, colleagues, fellow citizens,
No more money, and no more power –
Only peace, peace, peace,
Shantih, Shantih, Shantih!'

As dinner invitations pour
On the Sage
Like confetti
A brainwave hits me:
'What about sex?' I mutter in his ear.
'Don't add unnecessary complications,'
                    he mutters back.

Published In The Streets Of Dhaka

for Ashis Nandy

Pretty objects continued to be admired until 1875 when the phrase 'pretty-pretty' was coined. That did it. For the truly clever, apt, and skilful, the adjective pretty could only be used in the pejorative sense, as I discovered thirty years ago while being shown around King's College by E.M. Forster. As we approached the celebrated chapel (magnificent, superb, a bit much), I said, 'Pretty.' Forster thought I meant the chapel when, actually, I was referring to a youthful couple in the damp middle distance. A ruthless moralist, Forster publicized my use of the dread word. Told in Fitzrovia and published in the streets of Dacca [now spelt Dhaka], the daughters of the Philistines rejoiced; the daughters of the uncircumcised triumphed. For a time my mighty shield was vilely cast away.

Gore Vidal, 'On Prettiness'.

Pretty, isn't it – sure he's caught you
On the wrong foot, Mr. Morgan Forster
Broadcasts his priggish amusement
Over cigar and port in the King's SCR.

The story travels swiftly – and why not,
It's suitably droll – to Fitzrovia,
Where poets moustached with Bitter froth
Nibble nuts and gossip in equal measure.

But all the way to monsoon-racked Dhaka?
That's a stretch! I should know,
I was born and live here.
Your pretty tale swinging into print
Under the bamboo, the banyan and the mango tree
Is the height of absurdity – isn't that your point?

Point taken. Now imagine the dread
Of a writer from Dhaka. Yes, a writer,
For *Homo Scriptor* has a local branch, you know,
And at bazaar booksellers' such things

As lyric verse and motley belles lettres
Peep out of routine stacks of Exam Guides
Like rusty needles – I too have perpetrated a few.

But your unsolicited publicity may well put paid
To the prospects of any pamphlet or book
Published in the humble streets of Dhaka.
After all, Mr. Gore Vidal,
You are almost as famous
As Vidal Sassoon.

Your word may not be law
But it comes close, in certain quarters –
Deservedly. In assailing the iniquitous
You never beat about the bush
Or blare like a bully. In my axiological tree
You are up there with Chomsky,
Honderich, Arundhati. That makes your snide
Aside rankle all the more. Now,

What are we to do, Mr. Vidal?
Stop writing, and if we do, not publish?
Join an immigration queue, hoping
To head for the Diaspora dead-end,
Exhibit in alien multicultural museums?

No way. Here I'll stay, plumb in the centre
Of monsoon-mad Bengal, watching
Jackfruit leaves drift earthward
In the early morning breeze
Like a famous predecessor used to

And take note too
Of flashing knives, whirling sticks, bursting bombs,
And accompanying gutturals and fricatives of hate,
And evil that requires no axis
To turn on, being everywhere –

And should all these find their way
Into my scribbles and into print
I'll cut a joyous caper right here
On the Tropic of Cancer, proud to be
Published once again in the streets of Dhaka.

From
The Gregorian
(1967)

Les Misérables

The weary winter sun cast grotesque shadows along the avenue. Autos honked their way angrily through the early evening crowds, on foot and in rickshaws. Barely visible behind the surrounding office buildings, the sun's crimson glow etched the western sky. I dodged an onrushing baby taxi and dashed across the street.

Already the queue had formed in front of the Gulistan Cinema. In fact, I saw no harm in waiting a little for the long line to the box-office to dwindle. It was then I felt the pawing at my arm, and heard the consumptive wheeze.

'Please, sahib! I haven't had a decent meal for days.' Another one, I thought. Can't seem to go any place in this burg where a horde of beggars doesn't alight like vultures.

This chap was obviously in dire need. His right hand was completely missing; both legs were twisted and tortured. His dull, sunken gaze reflected want and misery, hunger and thirst, hope and hatred. His cheek on the right sunk into cavity, and the left cheek, if there had been any, would likely have done the same. Instead, a hideous gash exposed broken and yellow teeth. A stench of putrefaction assailed my nostrils.

'What a mess! Must have some horrible disease,' I said to myself. My face must have shown my own pity and revulsion. The poor wretch jabbed a shaking hand at my chest.

I felt my pocket. Nope, just as I thought, no coins. Just three precious single rupee notes, barely sufficient for a ticket to the movie and a cup of coffee afterward in the Baby coffee-shop. And, how I had saved and waited for two weeks to see this show!

My fingers withdrew from my pocket. I scowled at the poor chap, then turned away. Wasn't my need greater than his?

From
Starting Lines
(Poems 1968-1975)

Initiation

Out of a world dyed green
They drew him with a look
That said there was something
Special on their minds.

His heart was like the drizzle
Trembling like a lace curtain
As they queued up at a chink
And offered to share their glee.
Blank-faced, he saw only darkness,
To a charge of innocence pleaded guilty.

But soon he stopped climbing trees,
No longer loved their tall view;
Peeped instead through every hole he saw,
Became a tangle of hooks
Crying for something to fasten on.

Two Trees And Time

My oldest picture postcard
in the hip pocket
of the pre-faded jeans
of memory
contains a lemon tree.
The edges are frayed
but the picture's still sharp enough
to cut through the years
like a stiletto. The tree
is just about dead, short, squat,
sheltered by a low wall,
with warped leaves filmed with dust
by a mad March wind,
roots nibbled bare by rain
and stiff as varicose veins.

There's grandma in a theatrical mood
beside it, planting a smart
thump with the palm on her chest,
above the shrunken cleft, where collarbone
falls to the first rib,
hectoring in the cracked hoarse voice
of an actor who has strutted and fretted too long
an audience of one small boy
somewhere outside the picture:
>'Look, ye miserable specimen of childhood,
>This old flesh still boasts of tough fibre
>That lets no lank bone show . . ..'

Her audience sat in the sun
quietly twirling red, blue, brown
ribbons around the ears
like the lunatic from whose pursuit
he nightly fled, feet drumming ineffectually,
into sweaty wakefulness.

Grandma's hair has long since
stopped growing in her grave.
A tall mango has replaced the lemon tree.
In the breast pocket
of the corduroy jacket of memory
is a recent photograph,
crisp, sharp-edged, but the image
in the middle fast fading.
At my window a pale-green plume
above a frizzled deep-green head
waves at another spring.
A minaret gleams
in Freudian splendour,
then fades with the sun.
Changing chiaroscuro:
leaf to leaf
          trips
smudge of shadow;
dew-drops
soft as a hint or flicked ash.
The light on the TV station
comes to life, blinking: off, on,
off ... I anchor my eyes on it,
now on darkness, now on light.

Pop Portrait Of A (Male) Poet

Crying as a baby
you learnt all about assonance;
and all about alliteration
as you stammered into speech.
The moon in June taught you to rhyme.
That was the beginning

of your end.
You always get your figures wrong,
count nine fingers on your hands
when your spirits are low,
eleven when they are high.
For lack of mechanical aptitude
you can't commit
the rape of the lock
and must ask a passerby
to unlock your door for you.

Newspaper editors don't like the way
you dance on the pages
of literary supplements
and disturb the flatness of the prose.
Publishers always manage
not to pay you in full.
Intellectuals shut their doors in your face
for you rob their precious ideas
and turn them into birds.
Girls who fall in love with you
fall out faster
than you can write a love poem.

And yet, as you wander about,
your hair anarchic,
eyes out of focus,
biting dirty fingernails,

though your pockets have as many holes
as there are stars,
though your heart skips every other beat,
though your wife won't cook your dinner,
though politicians won't buy your slogans,
though students read your poems in paraphrase only,
though your clean rhymes hide dirty thoughts,
though poetry is never as good as a thriller,
you look great,
you're groovy.

A Poem In Two Versions

1. Sunset Song

The sun goes down, a luckless balloon,
Leaving a spray of gold in the air.
Patches of city sward,
Houses, new and old,
Even slums, even the crow jerking homeward
Wear a robe of gold
As it explodes over the horizon's brink.

Quick, children! run
Through the ruins of the sun,
Catch the gold in your hair;
It's fast fading with the light,
The huge glowing sky will soon shrink
And frame in black the window of night.

2. Tropical Sunset

The sun goes down
    A luckless balloon
        Leaving a spray of gold in the air

Quick, children, run
    Through the ruins of the sun
        Catch the gold in your hair

For soon it will fade
    And the sky will shrink
        And frame the window of night

Park

Nature on a leash;
indifferent collar of bricks
pierced by gates.

Like its kinsmen,
zoo tiger and pet dog, yet unlike:
one in irritation paces,
the other in contentment prances,
but the park in lonely introspection wraps itself . . .

Late morning. Busy self-centred birds;
A few human figures
like bare winter trees.
Voices: coarse rustle of autumn leaves.

Busy afternoon:
Throngs of bare feet,
            sneakers,
            leather shoes,
            high heels,
            slippers
press the grass.
When the lamps appear most are home;
a few linger
making hard park benches their couch,
the grass footrests,
the park their parlour.
At last they leave,
wrapped in its torn blanket of darkness ...

So I mused
on a lonely park bench
till he came and drove me away:
a gaunt fellow
with a munching beard
carrying peanuts and body-odour.

January 1968

87

Crackdown

A roadblock of uprooted trees
like extracted teeth of monsters.
In secret shadows your love
hides a bruised mouth. Bullets
strip the bark off the tree
you grew up watching grow. You would find
meaning enough in palm-fronds on a bright coast,
a moment of trance, a woman bathing
in the dark waters of the moon. That
has clotted, growing thick with dull terror.
You squat on night's shoulder
and feel it thicken into an uneasy hump.
And you are the night, a wandering camel,
smelling through contrary winds
the gun-barrel of a water-hole.

1972

Bangladesh '71

Venturing at last to go out
I blink at the guilt in the eye
And fumble with the throat
As if there were a tie.

Smoky dusk falls like fear
Over stone and human heart.
How, and with what, shall one create art?
Flames, death, then ash consumes the fire.

Blood of the doomed stains our sleep,
Like a question hangs pen over paper,
Fumbling fingers miss flesh they look for,
My love is vapour, but I don't weep.
Dawn stirs like a mouse; whose knock is it on the door?

Saidpur Cantonment, 1972

Consolation

No rude sun, a liquid sky
on the verge of tears, and only
moans from trees –
we are luckier than this world!

Baby

I nudged his face, smelling Baby Powder and saliva.
It creased into a toothless smile. At further excitation
gushed bubbles of laughter, reinforced by the strength
of a smooth, rounded belly. Then a lull
in our intercourse that snapped abruptly
as a warm, fast-cooling deluge burst around my waist.
An instinct to save my clothes reacted
in a swift arc of motion, left him dangling
an inch from the floor, wrist stiff in my grip –
for only a moment: your arms swooped down like a hawk,

swept him out of my hand, clutched his terror
against your soothing curves – and I
alone in my wetness. Your eyes shot reproach,
each sleek curve of eyebrow an executioner's sword
that loomed over my head. I groped forward
on eyes and fingers in mute explanation: I was fond –
truly fond – of him, your baby cousin.
Though in winter's midst, at his warm, flabby touch
I could already hear spring's first warm whiff
eddy around a lonely silver foil
from some dismembered cigarette packet.
The words poised on my tongue
like divers on a springboard; but your bright glasses
now grown into stern walls of accusation,
I could not speak.

1970

Pastoral

A horizon of green hamlets receives the sun
Without raising an arm or stirring
Into its lap, to lie there like a peasant
Untroubled by dreams and happy
As the coiled fibres of his muscles unwind.

Open hearths blaze into life
Diffusing heat through moonless air;
It stops short at my feet
Warming a blade of grass near a toe-nail.

Shouts of children move homeward
Like fingers clenching; their rags brush
Past me like fly-whisking tails.
The earth sinks as stars burst into sight.

Like a mollusc it begins to feel its way toward
Midnight and the warmth of a woman's body.
Cast out of home in seas far south
A breeze comes uncertainly to roost

In branches no longer fresh green,
And as it passes this patch of turf
Plays affetuoso on my string-less heart.

Night Is

a cat
        that softly purrs
& grows fat

an epicene
        that sniggers
at furtive lovers
        & nightwatchmen

an odd crow
        jerking its way
through muddy skies

the day
        that has been –
fractured moments
        defying glue

the growling dog that
        chases the cat
that ruled the alley
        when night was young

the dog
        fast asleep –
a heap
        of breath
in the doorway

a pair
        of empty shoes
an end-
        less yawn

a ling-
        ering
false
        dawn

Aubade

for Botu, Kashi, Moody and Faki

A clear cool morning green and grey.
Paintless whores plod slumward to wash.
The muezzin calls the devout to pray.
Time to sleep but there's no rush.

One drop more will do no harm
Watching the advent of daylight's monotone.
The first rickshaw bell acts like balm
When the world's waking and one's alone.

The newsboy's brisk shuffle strikes the note
A million instruments will soon take up.
I don't stop him; I know it all by rote.
To all problems my answer's a hiccup.

Nearing the dregs I feel as if
The wooden chair were a cushion of air;
I wouldn't swap it for Caliph
Of Damascus, full of worries over his heir.

The decibels increase as the men and machines
That make up the infrastructure of politics and murder
Rev up. Neither with them nor for sit-ins,
I grab the table's edge to rise for bed, slip, pass under

And out in a clumsy hunk
Of inert flesh, like any common drunk.

1975

94

Monsoon Rain

Dawn lay smothered in cradle,
Carcass bloated, spreading
Universal grey, gathering the day
In a heap of unvarying hours.

Over flat rooftops, unendingly,
Raindrops prick nipples of water.
Beneath his umbrella, a passer-by
Crouches like a hard-pressed boxer.

Inside, fenced in by vague shadows,
The easy key to survival: wallow
In boredom's porridge, dreaming of
Calm lands bristling with crisp sunshine.

1969

Arriving On A Weekend

After miles of smoke, then longer miles
of country dust, the eyes smart.
Foot-borne, they hug the road:
the wind squarely meets the skull.
A familiar voice shouts
a greeting. The sun
wobbles on water, then draws the curtain
behind tall bamboo. Released from day-glare
pools return each glance, glitter darkly,
like eyes flushed with malnutrition.
A few fish shiver, as if at a snake's touch.
Ripples circle, miming the horizon.
Where air played in transparency –
through interstices of reeds, bushes,
frizzle-headed trees, the mucous of night
thickens to chime of crickets.
Frail huts squat on the callused breasts
of ancient earth, thatch drooping
like limbs of cattle slung from cranes.
Each step into a depression
registers on the spine a jar
marking erratic time
beneath febrile stars. Arriving means
twisting around clumps of bamboos,
their sterile swish loud in the air,
skirting crude fences, missing
a rat's tail by a split second,
cutting across red rays from kerosene lamps
trickling through pores of bamboo walls,
through warble of rote-learning voices
harnessed to a dumb will, anchored
in dank ringlets of time-honoured truth,
And arrival means my dull footsteps
on the dung-plastered yard announcing
presence. The gathered ears are tuned

to a transistor's trill, each individual mouth
delighting in a shared hookah's smoke, in
intermittent therapeutic chatter:
crop-talk, cattle-talk, talk of power,
.of inscrutable disasters,
of death burgeoning everywhere,
incubating fast within parched ribs.

1970

Idle Hour

Dahlias sway in self-absorption
weaving without care
a skein of longing
at tea-time,

heeding not at all
in their unearthly repletion
impromptu birdsong or sun's
proffered ketchup,

mandrake's desperation, nightshade's
melancholy or their human
votaries; content
just to be

without having to choose
from madness, badness, sadness.

From
A Little Ado
(Poems 1976-1977)

Street Incident

Daintly she stepped out,
raised six inches
heavenward
on shiny stilettos

The breath of a furnace, the reek
of masses, expression-
istically contorted bodies
violated her refined senses.

Hellish, she whispered
in a husky contralto,
taking the unbearable strides
between air-conditioned car
and air-conditioned store.

The beggars thrilled
at the divine, imported fragrance –
and louder chanted
high praise of heaven.

A Myth Reworked

His father bought him a kite, a kite in Tri-colours,
with paper frills and paper cut-out of a man
pasted on. It was a man with gold buttons on his sleeves
and wings of a bat. 'Batman! Batman!' he cried and capered
as the kite had just time enough to lift off and see-saw once
before he was dragged away to be washed for school.

School was an old, fat, ugly man
and a lady, not young, not old, and full.
He told them in a voice deep as God's
of clever Daedalus who fashioned wings
with bird feathers and wax
to escape from prison with his son, his stupid son,
Icarus, who didn't listen to dad
and flew too close to the sun,
so the wax melted, scattering the feathers –
served him right, the feather-brained son:
he plunged into the sea and drowned.

The lady's backside jiggled when she walked,
her breasts bounced like a yoyo when she sat down,
and swung like a left hook when she turned
from the black-board and caught his eyes escaping
through the window to climb a string to the bright red
and black square of a kite pasted high in a corner,
like a stamp, on the blue envelope of the sky.

She piped like an alto saxophone
stern words that warned and cajoled,
words, words, words that exploded about his ears,
stories of reckless boys plummeting earthward
because their kites wouldn't buoy them up
when they lost their footing on the cornice.
He mustn't be one of those foolish ones,
he owed it to his family, his nation,

102

his own sense of responsibility, etc.,
etc., and then the bell

rang, emptying his ears and mind of all
save thought of kite and wind and sky.
Creeping away to the rooftop after tea
he tossed his friend up to feel the breeze
letting string slide smoothly from the spool.
Thinking of Icarus and unlucky kite-fliers
he lifted himself gingerly over the parapet
to the cornice, holding on with one hand
for support – he wouldn't fall, he was sure,
he was a wise Icarus. The kite shot up,
up, up as ah! ohms of sweet sensations shot
through the nerves. The world became a million
million strings of electric guitars.
He hummed in accompaniment;
but just a snatch,

stopped short
by a brick coming off in his hand.
The cornice hit his head, the string snapped
and Batman swayed drunkenly downward to earth.
He bounced off and slid through leaves
that rustled merrily and didn't moan,
a stump of branch stabbed his ribs,
the clothesline tried
to slice through his young flesh.
And when he came to rest
he didn't know himself
from the soft
cold earth.

Calcutta 1971

Puffy with premature age,
The buttons all broken,
Threatened at the seams;
Only the brown belt of the Hooghly
And the stitch of tramlines
Hold back the bursting.

Durga Puja

After the rains the flood goes into reverse
The sky opens into a huge blue parachute,
And Mother Durga descends upon earth
With ten arms to collect her annual dues.

Banias enter her in a beauty contest,
Debits are etched on the faces of *babus*,
Women grow edgy frying sweets for devotees, vagrants
And brahmins humming mantras in a stupor.

But where the festival earns its name, *shehnais* and *dhols*
Go into orgies, boys for once can jostle girls
With impunity, and every year there are more children
Sporting the unchanging smile of the unconcerned goddess.

Master Babu

He doesn't talk, he converses
or (better still) engages in conversation.
If his pupils indulge in it in class
He doesn't ask them to shut up or keep quiet
But to maintain silence,
Which, he maintains, is golden,
And in a torrent of words explains why.

Dog-eared as the edition of *Nesfield's Grammar*
Clutched in one hand, he walks home
At day's end through fetid streets,
Jostled by other people's cares,

Partakes of a repast of rice and dal
Before an evening of private tuition:
Making the rounds like a GP, dispensing
Extra doses of parts of speech to those
With faulty powers of assimilation.
It makes both ends of the day
Meet at dinner. But, 'Where's your son?'
The mother can't answer.

He ambles in at dinner's end.
'Where have you been, may I ask, if you allow
It is not presumptuous of me to do so.
I see you have the impertinence to maintain silence.
When will you begin to partially
Shoulder family responsibility?'
The mother starts to sob.
Howlers appear –
'Stop you from crying,
I am conversing him on crucial thing' –
And multiply ...
But midnight imposes a kind of resolution;
He goes to bed mumbling to himself –

As if it were a balm – words in the acquired
Foreign tongue, his precious bread-without-butter.

At times freedom from care does come to him,
Like an empty paper bag blown down the street
That snatches at the legs, touches a moment, and is gone.

Eleven Serious Warnings

for Hafeez and Nisar

Don't
    fall in love
        love is bottomless
        you'll fall right through
        and out into hate despair frustration
        or something worse
            like marriage

Don't
hate
    there's too much of it around already

Don't
    escape from love and hate
        into debates on delicate points
        of parliamentary procedure
            a coup will make you look silly
    besides
        some chaps are always saying
        objective conditions are just right
        for a revolution
            what if they're right

Don't
    try to bring about
        a revolution overnight
            even the earth takes a whole year
            to complete just one

Don't
    say with a shrug
        the very nature of a modern
        semi-feudal semi-capitalist
        tropical ramshackledom

with its economic tight-rope walking
explains the violence and hunger
and political somersaults
    the flushed eyes of children
    no god will save
    will want another explanation

Don't
    look for answers in books like
      Existentialism Made Easy
        life will give you failing grades
    or books like
      Teach Yourself Dialectical Materialism
        you'll get invited to
        Moslem weddings of Communists

Don't
    go Left
      the Right will fight you

Don't
    go Right
      the Left will yell
        you're wrong

Don't
    say Centre
      you'll get caught
        in the cross-fire

Don't
    drink too many cocktails
    in your angst or whatever-you-call-it
      alcohol is inflammable
        you'll become a molotov cocktail
    and if you can't help it
      don't smoke

or go near a smoker
or try to help your wife (in case
you ignored the first warning
and acquired one) in the kitchen
and finally

Don't
take any of these warnings seriously
for no matter what you don't do
you'll remain as you are
hanging
like washing
a woman has forgotten
to take out of the rain

Love Is

        simple
as a sum
        of addition
on two fingers

        complex
as a computer's
        binary
manipulations

Growing Up
or Softly Falling
for Sister Kathy

There are things
one is born to,
like ducks to water
or an eskimo to his blubber breakfast.
People of this sub-continent
squat or sit cross-legged
with an ease occidentals
can only painfully acquire.
There are people squatting
on riverbanks, backyards, rice fields,
cross-legged on cinema seats, football fields,
yogis squatting on Himalayan glaciers,
fakirs under a banyan tree ...
One of my earliest memory post-cards
shows me squatting in a field; another
shows me sitting cross-legged. Someone
might have pushed me as I squatted
and I broke my fall
rolling backwards, then got up
and sat cross-legged on the grass.
God in those days
was a benign giant,
the sky
a pocket in his shirt,
the stars
coins that jangled when he danced.

In missionary school I learnt to sit at a desk –
with cramped back, sleeping legs and stiffening neck –
sniffing civilization between two covers.
My chi-chi made me
a citizen of the world.

Besides nursery rhymes and ribald limericks
I learnt the world was charged with the glory of science.

A friend read me
a discreet article by a Nobel laureate.
It said the universe was probably
expanding, that is, scattering through space.
Like what? I asked. Leaves?
Petals? Pollen?
Seeds? Or is it like
sterile grains of sand?
Such questions make no sense.
The theory only asserts
        with a *perhaps*
what figures and telescopes indicate.
Well, I know for sure
        things scatter
through space and time.
My friends in shorts
wear trousers in other cities,
watch lovers talk in private
in public gardens, drink beer,
lift lonely mini-skirts on lucky nights.
Loneliness is the same
in Frisco or Soho,
Timbuctoo or Tokyo,
Delhi or Dhaka,
and so is love
and the enemies of love.

Marking time in this unquiet corner
I too scatter;
schizoid,
split
between this and that,
between my western know-how
and eastern wisdom,

between that and this,
forever falling
between two silly
stools in a proverb,
on the road towards being
nothing,
always becoming
something
that will never be me.

Turning with a pendular swing
away from the city
I squat on a grassy bump,
one of millions,
    (a British Airways jet goes like a needle,
    its vapour trail threads
    stitch nothing to nothing)
but I am singular in American jeans,
smoking an English briar.

From A Travel Diary

for Freddy, Paul and Rupen

An Artists' Village, a Crocodile Farm,
then Mahaballipuram. Finally,
stunned and sopped
by heat and humidity,
a beach resort
of huts and cut-throat prices.

All three are democratically described
in the same bland tourist-brochure prose.
But Mahaballipuram is the thing, the pride
of Tamil Nadu's Archeology Department:
monolithic temples
in the capital of a grand empire.

The altars of a promiscuous pantheon
no longer attended by ascetic monks
are shared half and half
with the goddess of modern tourism.
One of her priests is our guide,
a happily middle-aging
ex-college lecturer in geology

expounding in four Indian
and two European languages
the timeless stories
sculptured in stone
(that Time has been nibbling at,
impartially pockmarking deities and demons),
at times throwing in
comments by art critics
and a word on rock formation
remembered from discarded lecture notes.

My eyes sweep out
from an ancient lighthouse top

over a fluxing,
flexing sea
far from this swelter.

Scattered around the relics
are fragile homes of wispy people
who live on these palpable memories
of glory, sellers of coconuts, peanuts,
Coke and cigarettes.

In the middle of a walled acre,
inside a brick-and-mortar temple
with flaking-off plaster
the shiny-as-polished-stone shaven heads
of bamboo-thin priests in saffron
drowse as they drone mantras
older than the oldest name for India,

reminding the doubting ear
that faith co-exists
with Bollywood hits
surging from a tea-stall transistor,
rival election posters, buses
carrying clerks, traders, peasants
(THE NATION IS ON THE MOVE)
lettered large on its sides).
Says a schoolmaster-reformer,
an adept at yoga asanas,
the rolling metres of scriptural verses
are keeping pace with jets and ICBM's.
The Vedas have gone nuclear,
he adds smiling.

In the tirelessly rising heat
the guide's incessant commentary
begins to sound like
the bubble of boiling liquids.

Only two in our party –
flirts or prospective lovers –
are unmistakably alive.
In the sweet shade of the sour tamarind
he holds a green coconut
to her giggling red mouth
and whispers into her ear
the coolest place is near
the Shiva-lingam in the next cave.
But it's time to leave.

On the way to the sea
in the dust-billowing wake of a bus,
a group of old men and ancient women
materializes. Pilgrims
trundling homeward from nearby Tirupathy,
a place worth a page in the brochure,
where religion weds twentieth-century
trade and industry. Rows of barbers
give each head the required ritual shave.

Later the agents of export agencies
collect the hair for natural wings.
I imagine a transaction,
say on trendy Carnaby Street: a Nordic blonde
poses as a sultry brunette; her Estée Lauder smile
rivals that of any stone goddess.

Homage To Robert Lowell

A friend gave me the news two days late
(Newspapers have lately fallen out of my favour).
Did you roll sideways out of the taxi when the driver
opened the door, the way it happens in a thriller?
I retreated into my room and scribbled long pages –
like bandage rolls – of *confusional* verse to wrap around
the wounds your lines point out like fingerposts,
but I can't toe your line, it's hard. All night
the bandage grew thicker, clumsier, and under it
the wounds opened and shut and opened,
intractable mouths crying out your lines.

Hitting It Off

You said you'd make
my battered heart
whole again.

You've lived up
to your promise.

thrusting deep with
the thread and needle
of your tongue,
cobbling the fragments together.

Spring In Dhaka

for Gary Philips

Hair on a bare chest
quivers like antennae
thrilled by the scoop of the year –
but it's only another spring

A friend in hospital imagines
his wayward disc has slipped back into place;
granny takes time off prayers
to talk of the bright printed sari she draped
around her pregnant twelve-year-old-frame
and mother, listening, flashes
a sixteenager's smile under a grey halo –
but it's only another brief spring

Street arabs with running noses
race against top heavy double-deckers
while fallen leaves eddying at street-corners mock
the idea of linear progress;
the tantrums of rickshaw bells become merry tinkles
till the midday sun floodlights
a full dress rehearsal for summer
and tinkles become tantrums again –
it's only another brief tropical spring

But when from a long nap
I wake to hollering of children in a field
it's cool, cool, cool
from the roots of grass beneath their feet
to Orion's tilted bed in a corner of the sky –
oh yes! it's spring once again

Letter From Hyderabad

Arriving early I give thanks
for the weather, cool as the inside
of a pitcher on a village girl's hip

but thanks given early are
early taken back as I come
to the granite wastes
that buttress the city
and sit and watch the sun
climb its appointed turret and hurl
firebolts in all directions,
especially mine.

Watching the bare boulders
firm on the earth
I had thought at first
of your breasts, bared
to my undeserving hands, a gift
from heaven – grace abounding
in the world of the fallen; the curved
rise in a distant corner
was an upside down mirror
image of your rump
rounding up to meet my loins;
veins of rock fastened
on the landscape
like your arms around me.

But how the sun turned
the perfect similes of morning
into lies! – where amidst them
is the rich tender floral
sweetness of bareness
of your love-
line-
ss?

121

Sweaty, desolate
as the granite wastes,
I look at a lone flaming
gul-mohur and think of you.

Homecoming

When I walk the moon-spangled street
to the labyrinth of slums and sewers
through which is my straightest homeward route
the night deals a hammer first
blacking me out. Persistent rumours
about the world
are once again confirmed,
Darkness is infinite
to the finite limits of cognition.
Men walk bent by a sudden
chill
while streetwalkers on rickshaws
flash dark signals of invitation.
Crisp leaves wander aimlessly around me
but I am clear about my position,
in the middle of a black swamp
where wrecked boats come alive with frogs.
Your bright arms hold me steady
cutting sharp swathes of light, carving deep shadows.

Self-Love

Every night is like last night:
my dinner starched my mouth;
I stiffened into sleep

but woke up again
in the entrails of darkness.

The walls of my mouth
were like the geometrically hard
sides of new municipal drains

but my non-Euclidean
tongue caressed them all the same.

Anon

There's no getting rid of him
or her, as the case may be.

Flip through any anthology
of prose or verse or worse
of any century
down to our own,
he/she is there

Every time I come across
him/her
I wish I didn't have a name.

From
A Happy Farewell
(Poems 1978-1993)

A Happy Farewell

Having run out of poems
I rifle through old note-books
tearing out odd lines, phrases.
'Aggravations,' I read, and beneath:
'Newspaper that won't fold.'
Enough to ruin the morning
halfway through breakfast;
it can make you sit
'knitting eyebrows' on the throne
while your envious eye glimpses
'Mr. Spider dangling,
a lordly sinister star
in his cobweb sky' –
there's an image with possibilities,
can't imagine why nothing
came of it. Time to step out
into 'irrespirable air,' blinking
in 'the extravagant light of these latitudes.'
Ah, what sonorous syllables,
they almost make you forget
the heat and stench in the streets:
'My city has halitosis.'
Hits the nail on the head, what?
But streets are preferable to noisy campus corridors,
the politically minded always up in arms,
the young sparks offer no relief,
their monotonous woodpecker beaks
'boring into boring theory.'
Over a cup of over-sweet lemon tea
and another newspaper that won't fold
I dream of 'tamarisk-green hills.'
Closer at hand, 'chance erupts into romance':
under banyan trees, behind flowering bushes,
youths and maidens in pairs break
into the gibberish of love.

What can one say to them?
'Is it not a monstrous miracle
that every now and then two young persons
should pause in their saunter
at a perfectly ordinary spot on a perfectly
ordinary day, and feel in unison, 'Why,
this is heaven and we are in it'?'
One could also draw attention to
'Blood of grass on lovers' lips!'
Nice semi-surreal touch, I think.
But what on earth's this:
'devious-deviant desires'!
Did I consider slipping into confession?
Or is it the first symptom of the classic ailment
whose victim is that ignominious archetype,
the Dirty Old man? More embarrassing evidence:
'Blush of acne on nubile cheekbones.'
Reading, I blush for shame
and note with a critic's interest
absence of subject in the following:
'whose glance of frozen longing
is an arrow pointing in the other direction.'
Portentous, and so is:
'demands payment in shekels of love.'
Nonsensical too, perhaps. But 'the body's
bouquet?' Ah! ecstasy beyond grammar and syntax.
What about 'blind catch-as-catch-can of moist tongues?'
Temporary insanity, that's what!
Thank God for a change in key:
'At day's end
swift tropical darkness
brings metaphysical terrors.'
I am back on the streets,
'riding pink elephants
through ammoniac air of dark alleys.'
I raise my eyes to a 'checkerboard
of lighted windows,' higher to

'the discarded light of long-dead stars'
and 'the moon, lidded with clouds,
like a mad eye, winking.'

Time to scurry home
for the 'daily disaster-dose on TV,'
the daily existential contortion:
'What's there to choose between Khmer Rouge and
Khomeini?,'
the blandishments of the sitar:
'the maestro's promiscuous digits
romping in a field of vibrations.'
The last notes die away.
'As 12 o'clock strikes
a voice says
there will be no tomorrow.'
Appropriately apocalyptic
as two millennia of nightmare
rattle to a close. Shall I
lock myself in, twist my legs
into the lotus posture, though
'loneliness clarifies nothing
but itself?' Or shall we, as the
thrumming of the deluge begins,
try to 'stop up the cracks
with our singing,' and look forward:
'Fresh leaves back in their assigned season,
lucent green, lemon.' After all,
'All art is born of nympholepsy.'
But no, thank you, no more
chaining impossible desire to verse,
however free. Let me be content
in my abulic watching
of universal collapse. As for anything beyond,
'The eternal requires no celebration.'
This is a happy farewell.

O Clio

If history is
a nightmare
let me sleep on –
at least it's unreal

Cosmogony
(After the 'Nasadiya' hymn of the Rig Veda)

In the beginning
there was no existence, no non-existence,
no space, no sky beyond,
no death, no immortality,
no day, no night ...

                    (What the heck!)

no air, no wind,
yet Something breathed:
Other than that, nothing ...

                 (What the heck!)

Darkness covered darkness.
All this was water.
Heat awoke the life force
Came Desire: mind's first seed ...

                (Thumpets!)

Poet-fellows poked around in their hearts
and found existence amidst non-existence . . .

               (Gosh!)

What was there above?
Power. Seed-planters.
What was there below?
Impulse ...

               (And caprice?)

But nobody really knows,
maybe all this is self-created.
If there's a divine milord looking down
from the farthest Up
maybe he knows.
Maybe not.

What the heck?
Let's pile up paradoxes.

The Leader

I promised him a running commentary
so Uncle hoisted me on his shoulder.

'That's him! There!' the crowd yelled,
'There! There!' I joined in

sighting through a forest of raised arms
a patch of white, a dot of black

and stiffened
in panic,

Uncle bucking like a bronco:
'Where? Where?'

Abortive Sketch For Erotica

The snake charmer charms more
than her dancing snakes,

he wants them put away
and a different dance to start,
bends his fingers into a hook,
large banknotes for bait

but she draws back
giggling refusal, glinting eyes

saying, 'Look at mine!' –
a stiff cobra in her hand

Two Monsoon Poems

I

The sun so killing days on end
Then the rain so sudden.
A wire snapping entombs me in darkness,
native element in this land
Of sal and swamp millennia ago;
Torpid tribes cooled their souls
In river shallows like water buffalo;
Lying still I reach back to them,
Mind blank, moist breeze winding a sheet
Of coolness around me. The limits of my body
Become the limits of my world.

II

The days grow long,
Are cut short by rain,
After night-long downpour
The sun is fresh as a groom,
Water stretches to the horizon:
Impenetrable hymen
Crinkling at the wind's advances;
Sunlight fumes over the ripples. The marriage
Of the elements will not be consummated.
We try to fish in the troubled water,
Reel in inedible crabs, sweat like dripping reeds.
Frogs croak in perverse joy.

Baby Talk

My sister-
in-law's
son

plump
to everyone's
satisfaction

servants report
has
actually shaped a word
in the language laboratory
of his toothless mouth

Everyone wheedles him
for a repeat
& he'll oblige
by & by
& follow with more,
they'll hang on his every word

as they work up
a rhythm
        (like hoofbeats?)

spurred on
by desire, anguish, fancy

vault over
obstacles of punctuation
                (kangaroos: every pouch occupied)

till
suddenly
the insidious tripwire is sprung

Language
is a
life-sentence

Peasant's Lament

Your name on granny's lips
    mumbled
put me to sleep
    sang in my dreams
                Allah

on hungry nights
    filled half the belly
the other half cried
    for you, to you
                Allah
I stole a chicken and fled
    your wrath in nightmares
but no one found out
    and I thanked you
                Allah
Five times a day your name
    cried from minarets
scatters pigeons from the corn
    and people knock their heads
proclaiming your greatness
    through grunts of anguish
                Allah

Father prayed to you
    to give rain
then to send the floods back
    while the moneylender
cursed him
    in your name
                Allah

Between failed crops he got me
    a grave's-length of land

with a bride, her cunt
        like a baby's fist
in your name I entered
                    Allah

That was years ago;
        soon I carried father's corpse
down the familiar path,
now I must follow

leaving behind a withered wife
her tear-ducts gone dry
and a brood of hungry rebels
but also some money

for your man the Mullah;
        when I'm dumb down below
your praise will still be sung
                    Allah Allah

My Village And I

My name's immaterial
and perhaps, so am I
but it doesn't matter
now that I've got you
by the ear. I mean
I can blab as I please
into your ear in this
lovely banyan shade
till you're cool enough
to go out again into the heat
and inspect whatever
you're paid to inspect.

When people rushed to mother
with news of father's sudden death
they found her howling already.
As his eyes were shut for him
I plopped out and opened mine,
carrying the dark brightness
of his glance, as boys on Sports Day
carry relay batons, one from another,
in this field before us. The tin shed
across its stretch is where
the three R's were caned into my brain.

Twenty bookless years haven't dislodged them,
as I prove whenever a letter comes
for my neighbour – quite often, in fact –
from a son growing dollars in Bahrain;
or I sell my vote at the Union
Council election, signing on the register
while others ink their thumbs;
or the fat trader cum money lender
tries to pull a fast one
with his cooked up accounts. Yes,

that is our school-house –
though a cow lounges on the verandah;
if the man who is headmaster
can teach there – or anywhere – it is within
its rights. Besides, the scanty mangoes
have ripened, and jackfruits have grown
fat as the moneylender's paunch,
so it's vacation time.

That rise – crowded with bazar huts –
to which you have shifted your gaze,
if you are going there, you can see
the river disappear into the horizon
beyond which is the sea.
Beyond the sea lie England and America
and Russia, from where nice things
come for the blackmarket. Look back
and you'll see our village
as I saw it entire the first time
having tagged along with Uncle
to sell grain. It looks like a cat
hanged by scraggly children for fun
with the river like a thick noose
around its neck. But the river too
will grown thin as the children,
when the heat abates and the rain
doesn't have to keep coming
to beat it down. It's then

harvest time. The village is flooded
with people back from jostling
on city streets. They tell tall tales
to keep spirits high on the shrinking land.
They go back before the chill
starts with abrupt nightfalls.
I burn my dreams to keep warm
a wife with child. The dead

would have been happy doing it,
for a new child is fresh joy,
but every month people come
across the river to preach happiness
is preferably childless, though permissible
up to two. This is our third
and I am sad – for the child
whose mouth will open with a cry
to swallow swiftly-falling darkness. Sadness
goes with the climate; I suppose
it agrees with me.

Unholy Sabbath

The river snakes round
And prays to itself

Trees have stopped
Suckling their leaves

The sun bakes our pillows
Into hot bricks

In the village of your mind
The only store is closed

Moon

Aunts in orgies of gossip
plough through mountains of betel,
outchewing a flock of goats;
I don't listen to them.

Self-immured, hands
to the head, elbows
on a creaking escritoire,
I've missed dinner to imagine
the real terrors behind rumours
that bite their own tails;

when suddenly the air
is tinted silver,
through the window a rain-washed garden looks in
like eyes prettified by tears,
on the river beyond a canoe
goes by with a glitter:

it's that ageless moron again,
the moon. You don't belong
here, I tell it sharply.

On A Street

Nanga Pagla the sky-clad one
Terror and delight of children
Halts the traffic to announce his name
Is Badshah Akbar, Henry Ford, Aga Khan.
Then marching to the department store
Stops before assistants can bar his way
And dismisses them with a laugh:
'From you I will buy nothing.'

Cousin Shamsu, Durzi

Hunched over an ancient Singer
without a patch of enamel – deliciously rough
to touch and miraculously efficient –
he occupies a noisy corner
in my memories of country holidays.
Thirty years is as far back as I remember
but he has been around longer.

On market days he is a merchant
lugging a dull shapeless bundle
filled with colourful things;
and a fragmented ancestral plot
claims seasonal attention;
otherwise the treadle pauses
briefly for lunch and stops
when crickets buzz *Time up*! for the sun.

Each time he rises from work and stretches
he is a little less straight;
I may live to see him turn
into a bow
with the string missing.

His shirts and trousers are over-size
or under – like the bodies
they are made for; they sell well.

Scholar

He pauses around the middle of a sentence
for breath and a connective.
At its end emerges
a simpering platitude.

Back home he balloons it
With cross references and quotes
into a respectable paper
and balances it on firm footnotes.

The style is mock-baroque.

Business

for Matin

My old school chum
    the magnate
With uncharacteristic generosity
    – for old times' sake –

buys me a drink
    and explains how
business is like riding a bike –
    either you keep
going forward or fall:
    any third possibility
it merely the pipe dream
    of spoilt intellectuals.

At night I dream
    of waiting to cross a road
when with a torrent of tinkles
    an army of men in pin-striped suits
carrying brief-cases rush past
    on bikes, my friend in front
waving gaily, shouting
Look, no hands!

Disturbance

The yogi from
the ivory tower
of his head-stand

makes bagpipes
of his cheeks
and puffs puffs

a redhead
ant
proud of her bite
is headed his way

A Freshman's Unsent Bilet-Doux

The warm length of your thigh
along mine.

Was it spring or mellow
tropical winter? Anyway

there were no sombre clouds
except as metaphor:
the ever-present thunder-bellied lightning-limbed
monster of politics.

A cheerful sky then, blue and bright
seen through peepal leaves shining
like so many coins
tossed by anxious lovers:
heads she loves me, tails ...
A tiny smile blossomed on your lips
and on the pavement
a flower-seller's buckets overflowed
with elegant tuberoses, friendly marigolds,
mystic-erotic roses.

Now all flowers remind me of you.
This is my despair:
so many flowers
and only one you

and only once
happy chance let me share
an all-too-brief rickshaw ride
with you

the warm length of your thigh
along mine.

Summer Morning, Warwick

the sun a milch cow
udders
            knock-
            ing
about
the room
                i grab
& squeeze

your teeth
a row
of empty bottles

            slowly
                        fill

Communication

She turned to me and said,
'Queen Elizabeth's personal physician
is a homeopath.'

The words were moist
with saliva mingled
with the warm taste
of singara
washed down with Flowery Orange Pekoe.

The soft fleshiness
of her tongue was in them
and the impress of
charmingly irregular teeth
as on a bitten apple.

They flew like dandelions
from her lips to my ears
then lay between us
and multiplied like *The Morning Sun*
coming off the press at false dawn.

Ephemera

Early morning plums,
Sour:
Saliva fresh as the dew on them

Clouds I cannot name –
Cirrus? Stratocumulus? –
Paint the afternoon air

Beggars outside the mosque:
Circus of cripples

Water rising like mercury
Under a typhoid patient's tongue

Tea on my tongue
Thick as the mud on the street

Or should I juxtapose the images differently?

Ephemera of an early-wasted life

Slippers

Distant thunder turns into the alarm
ringing. Eyes open and shut
open and shut, each time making
new shapes, new colour.
Green hills and pink clouds on sheets.
Brown arms sprout from shoulders,
knotty fingers from hands. They lift
the blue mosquito net. At once
a pair of legs complete with feet, toes
swings through, lands on the floor.
Eyes follow but land on slippers
instead, and stay there. Poets
given to fancy might compare them
to the arms of a bride waiting for the groom,
to twin-ponies of a chariot,
to wings ready to take off.
I feel a shiver; it isn't the cold floor:
they're worn so thin, my old rubber flip-flops.

Surreal Morning

i say to my soul wake up you arsehole
crows are cawing apocalyptically in the blighted mango tree
the first dishcloth of day is wiping my eye.

i say to my body put your act together
roll, loll a minute or two on mauve grass
feathers from the Bay feel the hair on my neck

now stand up walk sit down
it's raining poached eggs
put up both hands, spread webbed fingers

let your eyes pick up headlines
& pass them to your mouth
let your mouth pass them to your ears
like a rugby ball

as usual they are reassuring & terrifying
PEACE TALKS ON
CRISIS DEEPENS
BANK FAILS
STRIKE CALL

Clock-hands move like rickshaw pedals
worms of rain wriggle towards non-existence

the sun appears with sudden clash of cymbals
plays with yo-yos of fire
bursting on impact on every square inch
unprotected by the sacred sign
of the invisible crooked finger
at the crossroads i step on a sleeping beggar
who lets out a musical fart & says thank you sir
the shutters of medicine shops move up & down like
guillotines
traffic lights blink on & off: blue, white, grizzled

155

traffic's in a snarl
horses on pushcarts
elephants on bikes
rickshaws on trucks
buses on human shoulders
i catch a traffic cop calmly chewing pan & stuffing
snuff into dirty ears
& hit him on his steel helmet
with an unbound collection of very free verse

lazy eels wriggle out of his eyes
i scream into his tinsel navel
are you happy with deconstruction deforestation
decolonization
depilation destitution demography

eh?

then suddenly remember if i spend so much time
negotiating the malibagh crossroads
i'll never reach the temenos at the city's edge
where a fez of a miniature hill

waves its tassel in the south wind
& the pure at heart can see

ancient hoardings advertising forgotten products
aspire to the condition of art

Poems in
Subcontinental English

Welcome, Tourist Sahib!

'Bangladesh Born To Tourism' –
    Title of Dhaka newspaper article.

When you come I go to airport (international Wing)
to receive you and conduct with welcome.
You are Very important Person, VIP to me,
full £ and/or $. I am BA pass
in History, Economics, Philosophy
and General English and Bengali
are the compulsory of course.
Now I training for tourist guide.
I practise in front of mirror (I have good-
looking face) what I say to you in English conversation.
I make vernacular conversation with local
and interpret and translate, both ways.
I have ambition for writing tourist handbook
and printing-publishing in Big Uncle's printing press;
I sell you with concession
if price payment is $ or £.
Guidebook to title *Welcome to Bangladesh*
and give our history, philosophy, economics, culture,
hotel list, places of interest,
foods of local delicacy, etc, etc. I will tell you gist now
before writing book. Bangladesh is new nation
with very ancient history-heritage, Hindu, Buddhist,
Muslim-Moghul, British, Pakistani,
Bangladeshi finally – and forever
we proudly confidently say.
With rural economics we are progressing
to industry. Our culture is rich
like television, cinema, dances and songs
(My love-life is cultural also
with neighbouring daughter going to cinema
and singing in bathroom – but that is personal matter).
To begin enjoyment of tourism you stay

in Dhaka hotel I suggest, Intercontinental
or International, depending on taste and budget.
Both have modem bathroom and bar for drunkenness
but former have swimming-pool
and ball-dancing facilities also.
Climate is no problem like Arctic or Sahara.
In summer you may like birthday suit
but that is for street madmen. You wear thin cloth
and our winter is your summer, so no problem.

Food is Western if you desire, but please try
local Moghul dishes – *biriani, chicken-pilau, dahi-barra*
and sweetmeats – *rashgolia, shandesh, chom-chom*
and many more to name a few. Sweetmeats give
sweet taste in mouth to take home
for kissing near and dear ones sweetly.
Many are the places of interest
like natural sceneries, rivers,
forest with Royal Bengal tiger and deers
(also monkeys) and longest sea-beach.
Also because of ancient history-heritage
we are in many ruins, two very important,
full of Hindu and Buddhist idols.

There are many mosques of course everywhere,
old and new, because ninety percent people
are believing Muslim religion.
Now conclusion of guidebook is coming,
I am telling something not in book.
We offer history, culture, sceneries,
not night-club, cabaret, sex as such.
We are for moral life.
But in tribal area I take you to see
men and women especially living naturally
in topless. Believe you me
they invent topless before West!

For final experience and joy you go Bang-
kok after Bangladesh. Before coming take this advice
personally and in whisper,
do not declare all currency at airport,
I give ten takas extra per £, five takas per $.
This is our philosophy: we believe in peace,
prosperity, progress. It costs money in foreign exchange.
So come. I believe in friendship also strongly.

Civil Service Romance
for Nissim Ezekiel

1. *The letter*

Subject: Improvement of Bilateral Ties

Dear Miss:

With due respect and humble submission
I beg to welcome you to neighbouring section.
I am coming the other day
early for a change
in view of new Boss
and you are also coming up the same stairway.
Power is failing as per schedule
and the lift will not move,
not even down.
Five floors is no joke for fair sex
but still you are climbing and smiling.
I am sweating but you are glowing
and becoming very beautiful.
Hitherto also you are pretty
needless to say. This is the face
I am saying to myself
to expedite launching of vessels.
Fair Helen, I am mentally drafting
make me immortal crew-member.
You are joining as Lower Division assistant
but you are Upper Division lady to me.
I was Lower Division also initially
and rose by dint of good performance.
I will teach sweet lady to follow suit,
I am thinking at once: how to do
the buttering of Boss
without compromising situation, etc.
By the grace of Allah my Boss today
is sending me with URGENT file to your section
and we are talking while the matter

is pending as per unwritten regulation.
What is URGENT when we are dealing
with MOST IMMEDIATE? Bosses and governments
come and go, but we go on forever.
We are learning family particulars,
likes and dislikes, making jokes,
improving all-round bilateral ties.
Now night is falling and falling
and I am like everloving film hero
tossing and turning with pillow
in lieu of beloved. I cannot find
further words, not even in dictionary,
so adieu. Please reply MOST IMMEDIATE.
I will die for you everyday
and remain

Your humble servant

2. *The Reply*

Subject: Matrimonial.

Dear sir:

With reference to your letter
of no date,
the matter is referred
to father through mother.
I am on casual leave
cooking dishes. Please apply
through proper channel
and thereby oblige

Your loving servant

Sahara Desert

I am Mr So-and so, I am so-so.
how do you do, Brother? It is pleasure
to know you for gossip purpose.
I am service-holder in commercial firm.
What is your walk of life?
Insurance salesman? That is too good.
You are enjoying life
putting fear of death in fellow citizens
and making percentage on premium.
Do you visit often this New market?
I come now and then
for viewing of girls.
You are married? No?
Then we are in same boat.
Viewing is our hobby.
But we are gentlemen.
Nowadays too many miscreant boys
are passing rude comment and jostling,
pinching and hijacking
and giving us bad name.
What is happening to world?
Ladies are like mother and sister, no?
Bad manners everywhere,
riot and civil war.
For this reason I am not viewing TV nowadays,
CNN, BBC, BTV, all full of pathetic news.
I want peace and quiet and love.
One day, because Father is dead,
myself will send proposal to choice girl.
God willing, after trial and error
wedding will take place.
maybe luck will fall on you at same time,
maybe we will have wedding on same date --
but not to same girl!
(But maybe to two sisters -- that is nice thought)

I will send invite to you,
you will send invite to me,
we will obtain motor vehicles
and decorate with flowers.
Band party will play film music,
we will receive hand of bride
together with many presentations.
But Brother, such sweet thoughts are too much,
they give me pain. O Brother,
what is life without wife?
Sahara Desert. Now is time for farewell.
We will keep in contact.
Keep me informed of progress.
Good luck! Adieu, Brother, adieu!

Party Games

Other day Bashir Bhai and his goodwife Baby Bhabi
are holding party. I am attending
together with myself and friends Ustad, Roy and Moody:
we are Gang of Four, I am thinking.
Our own goodwives are with respective families,
therefore we are temporary bachelor.
The guests are coming little by little,
everybody respectable and highly occupied:
Government service, NGO, business, industry.
Some are notorious also
but I will not backsidebite.
A few foreigners and non-resident locals
make evening most cosmopolitan.
At first we are friendly but stiff,
then host is pouring drinks.
We get tight,
loosen up,
let it all hang out,
everybody talking altogether
about everything under sun (and moon also):
'Greenhouse effect is coming.'
'Economy is deteriorating.'
'But Government is taking steps.'
'Yes, in wrong direction.'
'Housing problem, servant problem, marriage problem.'
'Palestine, Somalia, Bosnia.'
'Poor Mr. Boutros-Ghalli, always looking
like he is shitting bricks.'
'Problem problem everywhere
so let's have another drop to drink.'
All the time the four of us buddies
are using both eyes to steal glances –
some slim, some not so slim,
but very nice on the whole.
Then suddenly everybody's eyes

are filling up with newcomer:
she is just like Mae West in sari.
In my mind I am calling her Mae East.
She is too good. But her husband
is looking daggers right and left.
This is not liberal attitude.
After all, what is life?
Bag of air with holes in it.
In short, nothing
without mercy pity piss-up and lust.
With this final message I am ready to depart
together with myself and buddies.
Then suddenly somebody is entering
magnetic field of Mae East
and losing control of his fingers.
Mr Mae East shouts, 'Piss off!'
Then bottles and glasses are running through air
and quickly our gang is down on all fours
galloping to exit.

Black Orchid
(1966)

Imaginary Love

Imagination dying,
      imagine
            love.

I invent your eyes:
      a gazelle leaps
            out of the dark.

I cannot speak: love
      like a fish-bone
            stuck in the throat.

The moon turns over
      a page, a new chapter
            begins, titled 'Silence.'

Silently
      I invent a word
            to fill the margin.

It becomes your
      body, your arms
            make waves of light.

You speak:
      daylight offers
            a lexicon.

Earth fills
      with meaning, I sing
            in my cracked voice.

A look in your eyes –
      love: words in a half-lost tongue
            struggling for utterance.

But the concert ends,
        you pack your bags, snakes of dust
                coil through the streets.

You step onto the verandah
        of my dreams like an angel
                doing step-up exercises

in slow motion:
        the sari's close embrace
                spirals up your lithe form.

I draw close,
        you vanish, leaving in the mouth
                a sharp tang of longing.

An early train –
        a gigantic harmonica,
                rumble of wheels

fading into demented muttering
        routs me from sleep
                into panic.

It's carrying you away,
        unzipping a dusty map,
                putting distance –

space infected with desire –
        between my mouth
                and your ear.

Your voice through impersonal wire
        is pregnant with another life:
                a new flame

or an old one rekindled?
            I remember your nipples
                        like Vitamin E capsules

promising rejuvenation,
            my tongue
                        dreams of your saliva.

You write: I can't
            call you lover.
                        I want to talk to you.

Seriously.
            Night noises: fan, neighbour's
                        air-cooler, gecko, dog, foxes.

My mind's a cauldron
            of seething images
                        of jealousy.

Love dying,
            imagine
                        a poem.

And love,
            old Lazarus,
                        rises again.

Metamorphosis

time, a wriggling eel,

impossible to grasp
except with tongs
marked *pre-* and *post-*

& yet
this moment,
this world, this pre-

post-
erous age
becomes so completely ours

as you slip
into my arms
& become

a wriggling eel

Metaphysics

Infinity and eternity
are contained

in the space
between our bodies –

such being the lesson
of Zeno's paradox

we conquer
these absolutes,

making nought
of the nightmare

of separateness,
by the simple act

of leaping into
a tight embrace.

'Drink To Me Only With Thine Eyes'

That's the aperitif
in love's feast.

Lips for hors d'ouevres.
The entree's eaten

with single chopstick.
For dessert, pectoral kulfis

topped by sweet raisins.
Then cheeses:

your right armpit's Stilton,
the left Gorgonzola.

And I slide down
for a drop of liqueur.

Black Orchid

for Sumi

After the monsoon:
the circling hawk's eye
mirrors water and green patches
that conceal scarce morsels.

I become the hawk,
hovering over
your body: skin
rippling with love-tides,

and the dark patch hiding
what my hawk's eye craves:
the omphalos of my passion.
I set to work, snip and shave

with manic concentration
till it's all mine to view:
Black Orchid,
wet with dew.

Then panic:
terribly exposed, my rare flower.
There's no end of men
on the prowl:

connoisseurs, hobbyists,
or just plain perverts,
I wish I had a beard
to cover it up.

Nirvana

Yesterday I went digging
for my roots in the library,
thumbing a fat volume
though electricity was off
and crotch and armpits soggy.

I read of the *Bauls*, long-haired
groovy wandering minstrels
who said Fuck to caste and creed
and taught liberation
through the equation: Nirvana

equals post-orgasmic beatitude.
At last I'd found
my spiritual brothers! I hummed
their songs, considered mystical,
sung to rich twangs

on one-stringed guitars
of bamboo and gourd.
And I grew speechless:
your buttocks filled my
inward eye. As they do now.

The Border

Let us say you dream of a woman,
and because she isn't anywhere around,
imagine her across the border.

You travel hunched and twisted in a crowded bus,
on a ferry through opaque night
lacerated by searchlights,

to this squalid frontier town:
a one-legged rickshawallah takes you round
to a six-by-eight room, the best in the best hotel.

But instead of crossing over you lie dreaming
of the woman, and the border:
perfect knife that slices through the earth

without the earth's knowing,
severs and Joins at the same instant,
runs inconspicuously through modest households,

creating wry humour – whole families
eat under one flag, shit under another,
humming a different national tune.

You lie down on the fateful line
under a livid moon. You
and your desire and the border are now one.

You raise the universal flag
of flaglessness. Amidst bird anthems
dawn explodes in a lusty salute.

Purdah

Kohled eyes
glance sidelong,
drinking
ice-cold beer.

Speaking Of Kama

On reading A. K. Ramanujan's Speaking of Siva

Before
>   hair thins on top
>   or hairline recedes –
>   a one-way tide
>   or grey appears
>   on the head, on the face
>   or *Good Lord*
>   down there!

Before
>   the spine grows brittle
>   and death levies a harsh tax
>   on your breath so you pant at every step,

before
>   the balls reach for Mother Earth
>   and knock against the knees
>   and a ball pen is the only
>   straight thing in your hand

>   there's still time to seek Kama.
>   Court his arrows like a foolish soldier –
>   that is the height of wisdom!
>   Panting in the dance – let's call it that –
>   of lingam and yoni
>   you cheat death of as many breaths.

Rising from a morning dip in a pond
Nanga Pagla is ready to face the world again.

>   His matted hair is dark, his flesh and bones
>   in supple union; it's hard to tell his age.
>   His balls are firm as a grenade

and the penis, neither shrunk nor tumid,
dangles like a pliant hose.

What does he think of Kama?
'I worship him
so he leaves me alone.'

The Logopathic Reviwer's Song
(2002)

i.m.
Alan Ross
(1922-2001)
&
Brother Hobart
(1922-2001)

logopathic, adj. *Nonce word.*
1. characterized by sensitivity to words.
2. (of words) characterized by disease or morbidity.
3. relating to the treatment of diseased words

The Logopathic Reviewer's Song

for Priti & Sudeep

Late to bed
but early to rise –
so much to do,

so many books,
so many authors
to get through:

so many loafers
on my daily
stretch of road.

A quick breakfast,
quicker shit
and I'm in my seat,

ignition on,
revving up,
then zoom!

And I'm upon a lonely poet
meandering across:
who does he think

he is, does he think
he owns the road?
A blast from the horn

makes him skitter.
I step on it, swing,
catching his leg

with the fender's edge
and watch him hobble –
no sense of rhythm: poetaster!

A sententious bore – progressive,
puritan – waves
from the kerb. I wave

back, gesture to him
to step on to the road
as if offering a lift,

then slam him head on
below the belt
and leave him clutching his groin.

Now for a wholesale massacre
of the novelistic crew,
men, women, gender-benders,

the whole mob of word-wasters.
Head on! Swinging right and left!
In reverse! I drive

like a Demolition Derby champ
gone berserk. Does it feel good!
Yahoo!! Vrrrooom!!!

And though by evening I'm tired
as the sun, I can't wait
for the next day to start.

I'm the greatest, the one
and only logopathic
hit and run critic.

*   *   *

Got to admit though
there are bad nights
and worse mornings

when the will flags.
So many computers
puking crap

by the megabyte:
one against infinity,
a hopeless fight

and I just don't know
what to do, just feel sad
as the last dodo.

Pebbles On The Beach

for Shahed Bhai

Ah, the sea! How, do I see
the sea? A forever retching belly,
the earth's phlegm, bile, saliva,
primal chaos

spewing every now and then
these experiments with form –
pebbles, of myriad shapes
and sizes,

small enough to place beneath
the tongue – like,
who was it, Olivier? –
and spout Shakespeare
above the roaring, rearing waves;

others just the right fit
for a missile-hurling fist.
But beyond such uses,
however diverse, noble or nasty,
these mineral miracles
of texture, geometry, colour,
born of cosmic tumult
and tempered by countless ages,

demand the artist's adoration;
knocked one against another
their modest clicks admonish
our garrulity,
                        counsel silence,
contemplation.

Weekend

for Anne & Bernard Bergonzi

Across the street from my study
a man in *lungi* and sleeveless vest
tends a tiny kitchen garden

kneading the earth like a masseur,
watering it like his own
body in the shower

and before going in
bestows a lover's caress
on a plump gourd!

I haven't written a single poem
I'd care to treat like that.

Darkness
for Alamgir

TV news time
The power snaps

What if there's no news tonight
Only a voice

Saying over
And over:

All is well
Please don't go out of your houses

Landscape

for Abhi Subedi

The flood has stopped corning in
but will it go away?

Like a basin with clogged vent
you cannot see it drain.

Water thickens on top
spreading vaginal odours:

can they reach the sky
now free of clouds

blue and so tall
it reaches beyond the sun?

Nature

for Didar, Dipu, Kocbi & Mudie

A man moves to the side of a road
simultaneously raises his *lungi*
and lowers his body till he squats
on heels, remains in that position
a while, then reverses the process
till he is erect once more
and with light step
rejoins the passing crowd.

The sun goes down
spreading tomato sauce over the scene.

Sparrows

'This sparrow'
        begins a poem by Williams
                that I've just begun to read

when I remember
        a poem I once wrote
                about sparrows,

'an early work,'
        a biographer might note
                were I famous

but I'm not
        and the poem's lost,
                spring-cleaned away

and no regrets.
        Still, I can still see
                those sparrows – two –

on a fever-hot
        afternoon on
                the cornice beneath

my window,
        chirp-chirping,
                twitch-twitching,

fucking
        like it was like
                shaking hands –

so natural – or
        saying Gimme five,
                and then they go

back to chirp-chirping,
        twitch-twitching,
                and I suddenly remember

a lost line:
      'Post-coital rest-
            lessness instead of calm'

and am ready
      to go back to Williams
            but, young woman,

I remember how
      you turn my eyes, lips,
            loins into sparrows.

Writers' Retreat

for Anne, Carole, Di, Eleonore

The first week of cheery sun, blue sky and fleecy clouds
we are innocents in paradise, eagerly hunt names
in books on trees and birds, go on long walks,
eat like horses, giggle like naughty schoolgirls,
then sit through Sunday service in a heritage church
admiring stone carvings and the sermon's allusions.
Some of us write poems about these things.

We don't notice the weather turning, and when we do
say it can't last – but it can – it does.
Indoors willy nilly we turn inward and find
nothing's quite what they seem, or not just that.
The local taxi doubles as a hearse;
depending on its role the driver hums
a chart topper or te deum.
The local Earl's a copper, and as we show
each other our things in verse
could take us in for indecent exposure.
The glen that spreads itself like a peacock's tail,
the river gurgling New Age music round the clock
offer other sights and sounds for our contemplation:
the ancient inhabitants of our basement caves
made up in woad set off on raids
screaming for blood. Gypsy players
pounced upon without warning
are made a display, hanged from boughs
where late the sweet birds sang.
A village lass wades across the river
staggering beneath the weight of a bearded
weirdo fattened on sack. Playing tourist
Queen Victoria mutters: 'Interesting.'

By the third week we've written ourselves out.
Some have begun to hallucinate,

nothing serious, just a couple of mice
traipsing across the floor, but once it starts
who can tell? The universe,
thought Bishop Berkeley, is God's hallucination.
I know what some maverick
physicists are saying, but isn't
our universe enough, and one lifetime
and one month in this creative monastery?
'What!' I can hear the lofty-toned jeer,
'Why such pusillanimity in the guardians
of the word?'
                                    Come off it, mate,
we've done our bit, prayed –
even the atheists and agnostics among us –
for Fiji, Zimbabwe, Kosovo, Eritrea.

Our mystic runes can't staunch blood,
our verse, however free, won't liberate
any nation, or mend the weather.
Soon we'll pack, lug our bags down
the corkscrew stairs, turning 360 degrees in the process,
pay for the sherry we've consumed, and bugger off,
and our poems will be on their way to jaded editors.

Hawthornden Castle, Scotland. June 2000

Writing Home
for Sumi

On this hundred acre plot
that pretends to be paradise
of all birds I have an ear
for doves and crows
whose cooing and cawing
is just like at home

I remember the frenzy of rickshaw bells

I shut my eyes
and imagine the weight
of your head on my chest.

Hawthornden Castle, Scotland. June 2000

Strange Pleasures

for Belal Choudhury

The last time we had prolonged
political disturbances (which
are regular as cyclones or,
in happier lands, carnivals)
nobody knew anything
beyond their own anger
or despair, shops were half-
shuttered, buses ran half-way,
a half-hearted coup aborted,
the sale of tranquilizers
went up, foreign exchange reserves
went down, and nobody bothered
to keep count of bodies sent to morgues.

Mercifully, phones still worked,
were kept busy with chat.
A friend rang to tell me
how people still tried
to get on with life, indoors
and out: one man wished
to have his ear cleaned, another
who made a living by satisfying
such wishes got down to work.
The client sat on a stool
beside a pavement near a crossroads,
eyes meditatively half-shut;
the other sighted like a marksman
along a thin steel rod –
on his concentration depended
pleasure and hygiene or pain and infection.
Not far away a few random shots were fired:
one entered the sitting man's ear,
came out his other ear, entered

the ear-cleaner's eye, ruining
for good his delicate concentration.

How the phones rang with our laughter:
politics affords strange pleasures.
But I ought to add
my informant was a poet
and poets, as everybody knows,
are not to be entirely trusted.

Your Excellency
for Ihab &Sally

I hope you will forgive my inability
to accept your most generous invitation
to join the noble enterprise
of your party and the people

After all you aren't short of poets
happy to be on your bandwagon
fiddling away
while . . ..

But then
I'm not a poet

As Eliot said to young Spender
one can understand somebody
trying to write poetry
but what on earth does
it mean to *be*
a poet?
Not his words exactly
but that's the drift.

Being,
you may recall
from the 'subsidiary' philosophy
you took to get easy marks,
is the grandest, most puzzling thing
the human mind has dreamed up.

I just try
to write poetry
which is neither a nation-building
nor an income-generating activity
nor is it,

as you vociferously maintain,
divorced from life;
it is not
if I may slip into metaphor
a deep-sea fish
studied by men with infra-red eyes;
it is very much in the swim
of things,
it jostles the crowds
even as it stands apart,
so
I can readily sympathise
with those who, mortified
by its inability to prevent war,
famine, breakdown, or
pay grocery bills,
declare
that poetry is all balls
which,
in fact,
is literally
true.

Balls –
Testes –
meaning in Latin
witnesses.

Poetry
may not be the verb
in the grammar of dissent
but by simply being
itself
bears witness
to the system of graft and kickbacks
that governs your world,
the graffiti on mud walls,

the meaningless morse of gunfire,
love that may hold steady, go flat
like beer, or keep growing in root and
branch,
hatred coursing like blood through
mean alleys,
the wind that picks the branches
clean,
the drama of fresh green,
the rejection
of your invitation,
the putting together
of words
by which it comes into being.

Ideas For Poems: A Letter

Degas: I have these marvellous ideas for poems and yet I can't write poetry.

Mallarmé: My dear fellow, poems are made of words, not ideas.

Still, even Mallarmé must've had ideas for poems before he fleshed them out with words.

Be that as it may, here're a couple of ideas you've inspired.

Recently, as I was yet again overwhelmed by a flash-flood of memories of delights we shared not all that long ago, an anthology in my hand happened to be open at F. T. Prince's well-known poem 'The Naming of Parts.'

At once I thought of a poem titled 'The Naming of Private Parts' enumerating the various portions of that wooded, lovely, dark and deep region of your anatomy: labia – majora and minora, fourchette, clitoral hood, clitoris, clitoral frenulum, hymen (long lost), vestibule, vulva, vagina.

I've no idea how to flesh out a poem with these, but just reeling off their names is so dandy.

And just in case you're curious, my parts include the glans, meatus, coronal sulcus, corpus cavernosa, corpus spongiosum, scrotum.

How exciting to imagine your mouth shaping itself around these … words.

The second idea was inspired by an epic, no less! While teaching The Odyssey I was profoundly affected by the account of the underworld. Odysseus sacrifices a number of sheep to the gods, letting their blood collect in a trench. Spirits come swarming to drink and, held at bay by Odysseus' drawn sword, hover disconsolately around.

Thus, I imagine, at the times of your monthly sacrifice to the moon, when we'd make love even more lustily than usual, did the wraiths of your old loves, thirsty for your intimate blood, hover, held at bay by thrusting flesh.

Now, that was poetry even without words!

Ledig House, 2000

203

The Graffiti Artist

for Taqi

Some years ago two new student hostels were built overlooking the busy New Elephant Road. As soon as the whitewash on the outer wall had dried graffiti artists belonging to rival political organisations set to work. First they just laid claim to wall space, by scrawling arrows and party initials. The work of painting giant slogans with a bold brush at those precarious heights was for later (the hostels are five storeys tall and the best place for graffiti is the space just beneath the roof). But for the time being, one of the graffiti artists (I forget from which party) left a personal message: YOU RICH, I AM POOR – WHY?

It's hard to say whether the copula 'are' got inadvertently left out after 'You,' or 'rich' was deliberately, albeit ungrammatically, used as a substantive, as in the collective noun 'the rich.'

Whatever the case, the tremendous force of the question was undeniable. Why indeed should one human being be rich (or for that matter beautiful, muscular, intelligent, etc.) and another poor (or ugly, scrawny, stupid, etc.).

No matter how you explain things, resorting to genetics, history, sociology, etc., the question remains a stumper: Why?

Why did *you* have to be born into a rich, robust or good-looking family and not *me*?

For days the composure-shattering personal graffiti flashed its question at the swarming traffic. Then it was painted over and replaced by the usual stuff. a profound, if naïve, metaphysical *cri de coeur* gave way to political clichés.

Strangely enough, none of my acquaintance remembers having noticed the short-lived message.

Itchy Hand

[a Garo Folk-Tale]
for KNR and SH

A man and his wife used to live in a lonely hut. Once the man had to go to a distant market, leaving his wife behind. It was a trip lasting several days.

On the first night of the man's absence, just as his wife was dozing off, a thunderous voice commanded, 'My dear, I want you to scratch my hand.'

The woman was terrified. Then she saw a huge hand, dark and hairy, thrust into the hut through a chink in the bamboo wall. She let out a shriek and fainted.

When she came to, she opened her eyes fearfully, saw that the hand was still there, and fainted again.

This was repeated several times. Each time she came to, the voice commanded, 'Scratch my hand, my dear, or else I'll grab you and gobble you up.'

At last the woman gathered enough courage to touch the hand, but drew back at once in horror. After a few more attempts she began scratching. The hand seemed to relish the ministrations of her nails. It turned this way and that, reached forward a little, then drew back again, accompanying these movements with instructions.

'Scratch around my elbow a little .... Now the back of my hand, ... Now a little to the right ....'

If the woman slackened her pace, the terrifying voice boomed a warning: 'Don't stop, keep scratching, or else.'

This went on all night and it was only as dawn quickened in the east that the hand withdrew. By then the woman was near collapse from fatigue and fear. She wanted to sleep and recover her strength, but the horrible memories of the night kept her awake. She couldn't eat either. The terrifying experience had ruined her appetite. She waited for nightfall in a state of nervous apprehension, praying under her breath for the hand to keep away.

But as soon as night fell the huge, dark and hairy hand thrust itself into her bamboo hut and again imperiously commanded her to start scratching.

This went on night after night. The woman, deprived of food and rest, grew pale and emaciated. When her husband returned, he was shocked to see the state she was in. 'What's the matter?' he asked anxiously? 'Are you ill? Since when?'

His wife told him the whole story. He listened with growing rage, then began whetting his sword. While it was still light he finished dinner, then hid himself with his sword not far from the door.

'When the hand enters,' he advised his wife, say that you can't scratch it properly if it doesn't come in all the way to the armpit.'

In popped the hand just as it grew dark.

'Is there a man in the house?' the terrible voice asked. 'I seem to smell a man.'

'I'm all alone,' the woman said reassuringly. 'But I can't scratch you comfortably if you don't stick your whole arm in.'

The hand came in all the way to the armpit. At once the husband swung his sword and severed it with a blow. A piercing howl went up as the hand vanished.

For the first time in days the woman slept soundly. In the morning, she and her husband went out to look for the severed hand. At the edge of their rice field they found a shrivelled *mari bidu* creeper, which is said to possess magical properties.

The Firefly

[a Hajong Folk-Tale]

for Anesh

Everything was then newly created. The firefly was sunk in sorrow because it was tiny and jet black. There was no dearth of colour and the Creator had lavished varied shades on diverse creatures. Why was he so niggardly towards the firefly.?

A butterfly was flying by. Observing the morose firefly it stopped to enquire.

'Why so sad, my little friend? Can I do anything to help?'

'No, thanks,' replied the firefly, and added curtly, 'It's my problem. You'd do well to mind your own business.'

A while later a bumblebee that was happily humming along stopped to ask why the firefly looked so sad.

'Because I'm jet black and not colourful, like the butterfly,' said the firefly.

'But I'm jet black too,' said the bumblebee, 'and I don't care.'

'But you aren't tiny like me,' said the firefly.

Along came a bee. 'Good morning,' the bee said. 'Why are you looking so sad?'

'I'm sad because of the Creator's stinginess,' said the firefly.

'What do you mean?' asked the bee.

'I mean, why has the Creator made me so small?'

'So? I am small too, but I don't care?'

'But you aren't jet black like me.'

'No, but the Creator probably made you black to serve a noble purpose.'

'Not at all, it's only out of stinginess.'

Then one day it was discovered that someone had stolen light from the Lord's storehouse. Everyone was stunned.

The Lord summoned every living creature. They came and bowed, one by one. All except the firefly.

Everything became clear. The creatures who had come to plead innocence bowed and took leave.

Since then the firefly hasn't been seen in the realm of light.

Only when the reign of light ends is its light visible. One can see it roaming the dark like one lost, looking for God – in vain.

The Distant Sky

[a Hajong Folk-Tale]

for Rafiq Azad

There was a time when the limitless azure of the sky wasn't at a limitless distance from us. In fact it used to hover quite close to earth, so close that at times one could touch it. And at night the somnolent sky sagged and came even closer.

One morning, when it was still dark, an old woman began sweeping her courtyard. The sky was so low that her head brushed against it. The irascibility of old age was exacerbated by the sudden contact, and in a fit of rage she struck out with her broom.

But a strange thing happened. The broom didn't strike the sky. Where the sky used to be there was only empty space.

When it became light the children who came running out of their huts were astonished to see that the sky, so familiar and close only the day before, had become infinitely remote. It never came close to earth again, lest it be defiled by the touch of a broom. After all, there was no trusting humans.

Short Shorts

for FA and SMI

Should a woman wear panties under short shorts? An existential dilemma! For men, though, undies are *de rigeur*.

* * *

Purify the dialect of the tribe? No just trying to clean up my idiolect.

* * *

A happy marriage is a bad habit neither partner is strong enough to break.

* * *

Good communication is ensured in close relationships by reminding ourselves that the opposite of whatever is said is meant.

* * *

Democracy is meaningless without nomocracy. Unfortunately, the millions who vote and the hundreds they vote for do not even know that there is such a word as 'nomocracy.'

* * *

The subversion of logic by rhetoric is literature; and philosophy is the subversion of rhetoric by logic.

* * *

As we squat amidst the ruins of all traditions, creation becomes *bricolage*.

* * *

The well-known Marxist critic Fredric Jameson came up with the sound bite 'Always historicise!' To which, following Nietzsche, Pater, Wilde, and one side of Foucault, I retort, 'Always aestheticise!'

* * *

The beggars on the streets are actors; the traffic lights their footlights. With their woeful expressions, their spectacular deformities, their carefully maintained sores, their laments, chants, ululations, they depict a broad range of human misery, and thus fulfill the same function as serious drama. But unlike their counterparts on stage they do not crave applause, only a few coins. Such modesty is exemplary.

* * *

Disorder increases in proportion to the efforts to create order. This is the principle of entropy, valid in the human world as much as it is in thermodynamics.

* * *

O to live on canapés and cocktails! – the Hollow Man's notion of the good life.

* * *

Importuned by disciples to answer these four questions – whether or not the world is eternal, whether it is finite or infinite, whether or not one exists after death, whether the soul is identical with the body or different from it – the Buddha maintained a resolute silence in accordance with the very sensible policy of keeping mum about what cannot be talked about sensibly. This was two and a half millennia before Wittgenstein.

A Bagatelle For _____

I know
you
know me

and you
know
I know you

but do I
know myself
or you

yourself?
If not
how can I

know you
know me
or I you?

So let's
start afresh
I say

Hi
You say
Hello

and now
that we
each know

what
we don't
know

let's smile
and say
goodbye

Zen Poem In Monosyllabic Free Verse
Presented At An International Conference On Meliorism
for Gill and John Carey

All
I
have
to
say
is
this:

Sh!

Bananas: A Live Interview
for Angus and Joy

Do you have a message for mankind?
Yes, and it's important.

What is it?
Simple – eat bananas.

Why? Because
a banana a day keeps the blues away.

Really?
You bet – have a banana

and see how good it feels.
Keep off bananas long enough

and you'll go bananas,
simple as that.

Isn't that too simplistic?
Certainly not. Common sense tells us

the phrase *to go bananas* came into use
because banana-deprivation was seen to cause madness.

*Does it mean anyone who doesn't eat bananas
is mad?*

Not necessarily. Other fruits
can serve as banana-substitutes.

Isn't that far-fetched?
Not at all. Fruit-deprivation in general

can cause madness, which is why
fruit or fruitcake

214

in British slang means someone crazy.
By now, thank god, many

have learnt to appreciate bananas,
including political activists, artists,

philosophers and sport celebs.
For example? I turn on the T V

and Pete Sampras in close-up
lovingly peels, devours a large ripe banana

I am thrilled, and really happy for Pete
for love of bananas precludes jealousy

and violent passions.
Always? Well,

under normal circumstances.
As for abnormal conditions

take the Cold War days. A Polish friend
visiting West Berlin for the first time

stares mesmerized at bunches of luscious
bananas – affordable too.

None in the East, needless to say,
where stories such as she takes back

of cheap, delicious tropical fruit
fuels discontent. And before you can say

Jack Robbins, the iron curtain's in tatters.
You've seen it on TV, swallowed the rhetoric

but now you know what was really on the minds
of the furious mobs:

GIVE ME BANANAS OR GIVE ME DEATH!
Makes you wonder about history.

And what about art?
What about art? David Hockney

has done some delicious bananas
and Kandinsky said yellow –

synonymous with bananas –
is the colour of life.

What about sick bananas?
Enough to induce dejection.

How melodramatic!
You may laugh, but I know.

A toddler in kindergarten,
I sallied forth one balmy morning,

a happy yellow banana in my canvas satchel.
Come tiffin time I eagerly take it out –

lo and behold it isn't there!
Instead, out comes one roasted black.

The teacher crinkles her nose:
'Bring nicely ripe bananas!'

How could I explain that's just what I did
and I hadn't the foggiest notion how

that sorry, limp black thing got in.
It was the canvas satchel did the mischief.

Of course, so let me urge you
to take good care of the health

of your bananas, just as they take good care
of yours. Why, they're even rare medicine!

That's laying it on.
No, listen, a lovely woman

I've had a crush on since '69 …
69, eh?

Nineteen sixty-nine, if you please,
and no pun concealed.

No need to get shirty.
She was in America and suddenly

night after night
Yes! Yes! Night after night?

She'd wake up in agony
from a cramp in the leg.

I know how it feels.
Finally she went to her doc

and he said … *Eat bananas …*
At least one a day

And she's been fine ever since?
And pretty as ever.

Lovely, now what about philosophy?
Sartre said that literature

like bananas should be tasted fresh.
And the literature of the past?

So much of it is like bananas gone limp
and black in the satchel of time.

But the old stuff that still moves us?
Truly great, blessed with magic ...

Magic that makes nought of satchels?
Has so far.

Not forever?
Nothing is forever.

     Ledig House, 2000

218

Trust

for FAH, PH, NZ

In the queue for paying the electricity bill the man behind me is nervous. The counter is still some way off and from time to time someone tries to inveigle those in the queue into letting them squeeze in. A brief apology is enough to rebuff them but the man at my back isn't so sure. He can't trust words and he can't trust people. He must secure his defences against inveiglers, and to this end tries to abolish all space between us. He hooks his chin on my shoulder, wraps his arms around my waist, and won't be shaken off–until I threaten to use Kung Fu.

And now I can't shake off the memory of that strange fellow who couldn't trust others. For I can't trust myself, and tingle with fear lest I should do something vile – pinch a swivelling bottom, suddenly utter vicious words only half meant. Or worse. Shrilling kites resound in my head. There's madness in the air. What if my souvenir kukri unsheathes itself in my hand and slices an offending neck, or my fingers slip a detonator into place?

I look at my quivering hands; wrapping my arms around myself in a bear hug, whisper 'Peace! Peace!'

Dear Reviewer

Right now I'm free
of the fear that plagues
all poets –
of not being read

for *you*
are read-
ing these
wobbly lines.

I don't crave awards
or such praise as humdingers
among writers receive
in the grave

but I do long
to be noticed
for (remember Bishop
Berkeley?) not to be
noticed is not to be!

Feel free to damn
with faint praise
or just damn me –
but in print, please!

I will read you in either case,
cut you out, frame
and hang you on my wall
for others to read:

yours is the superior art,
giving book news
fortified with smart views –
you go down like a small sherry.

And just in case you are
in a good enough mood to say
'The value of this work will surely
keep pace with paper prices,'
why, I'll feel I'm immortal!

Signed: Illegible.

Appendix

An Apology for Bangladeshi Poetry in English

Ever since subcontinentals started doing creative writing in the late 18th century they (especially the versifiers among them) have faced the question, 'Why write in English and not your mother tongue?' One can answer the question broadly by saying that if a language is taught and used in a region, some are bound to try creative writing in it. But each writer has a personal story to tell.

I do not think I would have tried creative writing in English if I weren't an English-medium boy. From the age of four I moved in three realms. At home in a poor neighbourhood in Dhaka I belonged to a barefoot troop happily at play in the dust, jabbering away in East Bengali Bangla, and spending part of my spare time in reading Bangla. At school, which for five years was Don's Kindergarten, run by a Eurasian family in tandem with the 'Hotel Airline and Bar' on the upper storey of the schoolhouse, I sat well-shod and strait-jacketed in shorts, tucked-in shirt and tie, chanting English lessons in chorus. We were a motley crowd of Bangla, Urdu and Gujrati speakers, with a handful of anglophone Eurasians thrown in. Until everyone had acquired Basic English the lingua franca was what I believe used to be called Hindustani, which was nearly as alien to me as English. I had been a garrulous infant. Now I grew tongue-tied. By the time I began to feel a growing confidence in my use of English it was time to move to St. Gregory's High School downtown, founded over a century ago by a Belgian Benedictine and now run by American Catholic missionaries.

During vacations I would move to my mother's ancestral village. Though only a dozen miles by bus from the city centre it was a fairy-tale world of birds and beasts, elusive *pretas* and rough-talking peasants. In summer we swam, fished, punted (with bamboo poles). In winter we played *kabaddi*, hunted foxes – not in hunting pink or mounted on thoroughbreds, but in a barefoot, *lathi*-wielding chase.

I spent two years at Faujdarhat Cadet College, set up with military patronage along English public-school lines. Among our English texts were *Tom Brown's Schooldays*, which all of you know and *Adventures at Dabanga School*, which no one here has probably heard about. Dabanga is a boarding school somewhere in East Africa, in a region where smugglers thrive. Among the students is a rough beer-drinking character called Nelson who becomes embroiled in criminal activities. But as events build up to a thrilling climax he reveals his innate goodness and becomes the hero of the hour. Despite the efforts of the Principal, a colonel from New Zealand, Faujdarhat didn't quite measure up to Rugby. It fell somewhere between Rugby and Dabanga.

But how did I get to writing in English – and poetry at that. I wasn't a great poetry buff in school. The great English poets – Milton, Wordsworth, Byron, Shelley, Keats – were names to remember and drop at opportune moments. But what we read by them didn't particularly appeal – a common experience in the tropics, it seems. Naipaul points out how English literature as encountered by 'us' is 'like an alien mythology. There was, for instance, Wordsworth's notorious poem about the daffodil. A pretty flower, no doubt; but we had never seen it. Could the poem have any meaning for us?' Once a friend got me interested in Shelley by whispering that he had written a poem in which occurred the phrase 'The golden tresses between her thighs.' A futile search in the school library followed. I still haven't discovered the source of this exciting line. If anyone can help I shall be most grateful.

Besides the flora and fauna there is the prosody of traditional English verse. It is alien to us. Just note how awkwardly our students read it. Their difficulty is exacerbated by the fact that subcontinental English, though an identifiable linguistic phenomenon, has not yet evolved a standard form—in the sense there is a 'standard' form of British or American English.

Then I had something like a conversion experience. Our literature classes at St. Gregory's were taken by Brother Hobart, a loveable Irish-American eccentric, one of the most remarkable personalities I have known. He would take a poem and draw the whole class into the exercise of producing a critical appreciation. What sort of poem is it? Who is saying what and to whom? What do the similes and metaphors say to us? Asking such questions, trying out answers, modifying them, he would write out a response to the poem on the blackboard. He taught me that writing was a process of playing around with words till one struck what seemed the right note. Moving from poem to poem in our textbook we came to Lawrence's 'Snake.' And it opened up a whole new world. I could feel the music of its free verse as I hadn't felt the music of any other English poem. Its simple diction gave me immediate access to the dramatic situation in the poem. It hardly mattered that I had never seen a carob-tree, which features prominently in the poem; the adjectival fanfare preceding it – 'the deep, strange-scented shade of the great dark carob-tree' – brought it to life. I started scribbling free verse. Walking in the park (this was soon after I left school) I began a poem, 'Nature on a leash.' Friends applauded. I began enjoying myself in my new role. I do not wish to make too much of this experience, but it may not be farfetched to hypothesize that similar experiences must be quite common in the Third World; the fact that most Third World English poetry is in free verse would seem to support the hypothesis.

Not long after I discovered Philip Larkin – 'Hatless, I take off/ My cycle-clips in awkward reverence' just bowled me over – and also thrilled to Allen Ginsberg's ecstatic chant, 'Kral Majales': 'And I am the King of May, which is the power of sexual youth'. I like to think that my work occupies the uneasy no-man's-land between the cool poetry of the

Movement and the vatic utterances of the Beat generation. But the immediate literary tradition I relate to is that of Anglophone Indian or South Asian writing as it has evolved from the late eighteenth century onwards: in prose, from Sake Deen Mahomed onwards; in poetry, from Henry Louis Vivien Derozio onwards.

By now the controversy over whether subcontinentals can create significant literature in English is a matter of cultural history. The ill-humoured attack by the Bengali poet Buddhadev Bose in an encyclopedia entry on Indo-Anglian poetry (i.e., Indian English poetry) is not likely to be repeated. (He described Indo-Anglian poetry as a *cul-de-sac* lined with curio shops.) But have the objections raised against it been completely refuted? At the heart of the diatribe lay the belief that authentic poetry can be written only in one's mother-tongue. Is this a totally wrong-headed view? I do not think so. It is pertinent to remember that neither India nor Africa, where English is not the mother-tongue of a significant fraction of the population, has produced a major poet in English, but the Caribbean, where a kind of English is the mother-tongue, has – Walcott.

Emile Cioran, himself a crosser of linguistic boundaries (he was a Rumanian who wrote exquisite French prose), comments: 'In a borrowed language, you are *conscious* of words; they exist not in you but outside of you. This interval between yourself and your means of expression explains why it is difficult, even impossible, to be a poet in another language besides your own. How extract a substance from words that are not rooted in you? The newcomer lives on the surface of language; he cannot, in a tongue belatedly learned, translate that subterranean agony from which poetry issues.'

Hard evidence of a sort for this view comes from the cognitive sciences. Steven Pinker in *The Language Instinct* mentions an ingenious experiment that shows how early infants get attuned to their mother-tongue. It was found that 'four-day-old French babies suck harder to hear French than

Russian, and pick up their sucking more when a tape changes from Russian to French than from French to Russian.' This positive response to the mother-tongue is due to the fact that 'the melody of mothers' speech carries through their bodies and is audible in the womb. The babies still prefer French when the speech is electronically filtered so that the consonant and vowel sounds are muffled and only the melody comes through. But they are indifferent when the tapes are played backwards, which preserves the vowels and some of the consonants but distorts the melody. Nor does the effect prove the inherent beauty of the French language: non-French infants do not prefer French, and French infants do not distinguish Italian from English.' The inference is that 'The infants must have learned something about the prosody of French (its melody, stress and timing) in the womb, or in their first days out of it.'

The experiment demonstrates that one is most intimate with the lyric genius of one's mother-tongue. It follows that poetry written in a language other than one's mother-tongue is not likely to be conspicuous for its lyricism. And this, I believe, is the case with Indian English and African English poetry. Dom Moraes of course was very lyrical, but his mother-tongue was English.

But it does not follow, as Bose thought, that subcontinental poetry in English is doomed to oblivion. The best of it is good by any standard, noteworthy for its irony and satire, the quality of its imagery, its use of the Indian voice. It gives us something one cannot find in any other kind of English poetry or in poetry in the subcontinent's regional languages. Besides, with the subcontinental diaspora more and more Indians are picking up English in their mothers' wombs, so to speak, and so the chances of a major Indo-Anglian poet emerging are improving with every passing day. In any case, as far as I am concerned, there is no getting away from the fact that my literary language is English. Writing is my vocation, and I must write in English, and submit to the judgment of reader and critic. Regarding idiom, I seek inspiration from the great Alexandrian Greek poet C. P.

Cavafy. Mutatis mutandis, I find my poetic credo on the idiom to use in Cavafy's poem 'For Ammonis, Who Died at 29, in 610,' where he addresses one Raphael, who has been asked 'to write a few lines/ as an epitaph for the poet Ammonis', and passes on the following advice:

Your Greek is always elegant and musical.
But we want all your craftsmanship now.
Our sorrow and our love move into a foreign language.
Put your Egyptian feeling into the Greek you use.

Raphael, your verses, you know, should be written
so they contain something of our life within them,
so the rhythm, so every phrase clearly shows
that an Alexandrian is writing about an Alexandrian.
(translated by Edmund Keeley and Philip Sherrard)

Part of my writerly activities involve translating from Bangla. This has a special significance for me. Since my literary sensibility has two rather distinct areas, one occupied by Bangla literature, the other by literature in English and literature read in English translation, translating is a way of unifying the two. It is also a means of coming to terms with aspects of myself of which I may have been only vaguely aware, and of combining the creative and critical sides of my mind: Pound, you may recall, cites translation as a mode of criticism.

My translations have all been labours of love: Shamsur Rahman and Shaheed Quaderi, dear friends besides being leading Bangla poets; *The Wonders of Vilayet*, an eighteenth century Indian's memoir of a trip to Britain; Tagore's *Chaturanga (Quartet)*. And Tagore's *Yogayog*, for which I am looking for a publisher (a few chapters have appeared in *The Essential Tagore*, eds. R. Chakravarty and F. Alam: Harvard U. P.). Generally speaking, I find translating Bangla prose a more satisfying activity than translating the poetry, partly because more is lost in translating poetry.

The prose, on the other hand, incorporates more of the complex texture of our culture and is therefore likely to appeal to readers interested in otherness. Doesn't Richard Rorty in *Irony, Contingency, Solidarity* make a case for novels and documentaries as the best agents available for broadening and deepening our human sympathies?

Translating Tagore's *Quartet* led me to realize with blinding clarity the extent to which the Bengali psyche – and indeed my individual psyche – is polarized between the devotional and romantic on the one hand, and the logical and rational on the other. We have all been aware of the impact of *bhakti* with its associated irrationalism and eroticism on the Bengali mind. We are perhaps less aware of our logic-chopping side, which goes back at least as far as the Navya-Nyaya logicians of the sixteenth century. It is conspicuous today as what Alan Ross in a poem titled 'Bengal' calls 'A querulous literacy.' The opposition between the two weltanschauungs passed into popular culture, as in the saying, *Biswasay milay swarga, tarkey bahudur* – 'Faith takes you to heaven, but arguments lead you astray.' I recall it from my childhood. In its original form it has 'Krishna' instead of 'swarga' ('heaven') and was obviously a *bhakti* squib directed at the hair-splitting logicians. By substituting 'swarga' for 'Krishna' muslims too could use the proverb: an interesting example of how the two religious communities could drink from the fount of a shared culture.

Sadly, the two aspects of the Bengali psyche seem to have remained separate through our history: ours has always been a dissociated sensibility. I like to think that in trying to write in English – an activity that, as Meenakshi Mukherji pointed out years ago, enhances our critical awareness of the complexities of our cultural inheritance – I also try to bring the disparate parts into a meaningful, dialogic relationship.